JOHNS HOPKINS AT THE AGE OF 40
From a portrait in the Johns Hopkins University

JOHNS HOPKINS
A SILHOUETTE

BY
HELEN HOPKINS THOM

THE JOHNS HOPKINS UNIVERSITY PRESS
BALTIMORE

© 1929 The Johns Hopkins Press
Published October 1929. Reprinted January 1930
© 2009 The Johns Hopkins University Press
All rights reserved. Published 2009
Printed in the United States of America on acid-free paper
2 4 6 8 9 7 5 3 1

The Johns Hopkins University Press
2715 North Charles Street
Baltimore, Maryland 21218-4363
www.press.jhu.edu

Library of Congress Control Number: 2008939359

ISBN 13: 978-0-8018-9098-7
ISBN 10: 0-8018-9098-5

*Special discounts are available for bulk purchases of this book. For more informa-
tion, please contact Special Sales at 410-516-6936 or specialsales@press.jhu.edu.*

The Johns Hopkins University Press uses environmentally friendly book
materials, including recycled text paper that is composed of at least 30 per-
cent post-consumer waste, whenever possible. All of our book papers are
acid-free, and our jackets and covers are printed on paper with
recycled content.

To My Father
JOSEPH S. HOPKINS
Whose Personal Reminiscences of
his Uncle Have Made
This Book Possible

The reprinting of *Johns Hopkins: A Silhouette* by the Johns Hopkins University Press, first published by the then-named Johns Hopkins Press in 1929, is made possible by the generous gift of an anonymous donor in honor of the history and legacy of the Hopkins family.

CONTENTS

INTRODUCTION TO THE 2009 EDITION

WHEN Helen Hopkins Thom wrote *Johns Hopkins: A Sil-houette* in 1929, it was the first book-length biography of Johns Hopkins to be published. Almost eighty years later, *Silhouette* still holds the distinction of being the only biography of the man who founded a world renowned university and hospital.

Johns Hopkins was a complex man, a walking bundle of contradictions. He entertained the "best and brightest" of his day, sparing no expense to ensure their comfort and enjoyment, yet he was reluctant to replace his own threadbare clothes and furnishings. He belonged to a religious denomination that shunned alcohol, yet he served fine wines to his guests, and he accepted barrels of whiskey in barter (bottling and selling it under the name "Hopkins Best"). He remained childless throughout his life, yet he enjoyed frequent visits from nieces and nephews. He never traveled far from home in his lifetime, yet the institutions bearing his name are known worldwide.

Despite these contradictions, the primary reason no one else has attempted a full biography of Johns Hopkins probably hinges on his basic humility. Although he was a successful businessman in several fields of commerce, he never considered himself more important than anyone else. He wrote letters in the course of his life, and received many in return. But, feeling no need to justify his stature to posterity, he made no attempt to preserve his correspondence. To the contrary, he disposed of any piece of paper that had outlived its immediate purpose. Consequently, he left no "paper trail" for historians to examine motivations or interpretations. Correspondence exists in the papers of his contemporaries, but those are scattered and difficult to track down. While public figures often tried to conceal their activities by disposing of evidence, Johns Hopkins considered himself a simple businessman, no better or worse than any other humble person, and therefore undeserving of recognition. The Department of Special Collections and Archives, in the Sheridan Libraries of The Johns Hopkins University, holds a small collection of Johns's "Papers." Unfortunately, aside from a family Bible, these papers amount to little more than scraps, with little that dates from the man's life.

We are, therefore, indebted to Helen Hopkins Thom. Based primarily on recollections of her father and other relatives, she wrote this biography of her great-uncle, published fifty-six years after Johns's death. Biographical sketches and magazine articles have been written since 1929, but no formal biography has been attempted. The historian will recognize that a narrative based on personal recollection may be suspect, both from a factual as well as an interpretive standpoint. Thom certainly made no attempt to depict her relative in anything but positive terms, and one may wonder whether conversations quoted over fifty years later, in the absence of written evidence, reflect an accurate record of the spoken word. Given the scarcity of written documentation, we must rely, to a large extent, on the honesty and humility of Johns's collateral descendants, in order to accept the quotations as authentic.

Helen Rolfe Hopkins Thom was a grandniece of Johns Hopkins. Johns's elder brother, Joseph, married Elizabeth Scofield. Their fourth child, Joseph S. Hopkins, married Annette Hopkins, and they had two daughters. The elder daughter was Helen Rolfe Hopkins, born in 1867 at Clifton, Johns's summer home at Erdman Avenue and Harford Road. After briefly attending Goucher College, she graduated from Bryn Mawr College in 1891. Her husband, Hunt Mayo Thom, from another prominent Maryland family, was an importer who was also involved in real estate, while Mrs. Thom was active in various social and literary clubs. Together, they raised three daughters on a farm near Gibson Island, Maryland, where her husband was an avid yachtsman and member of the Baltimore Yacht Club. Hunt Thom died in 1925, four years before *Silhouette* was published. Mrs. Thom lived as a widow in Baltimore until 1948, when she died in her home on Eutaw Place at the age of 79. While she recalls in her Foreword visiting her great-uncle as a child (she was six years old when Johns died), most of her knowledge of her subject necessarily came from her father, uncles, and aunts, who knew Johns as children and then as adults.

Despite Johns Hopkins's deep humility, he definitely is worthy of a biography. Forced to leave school at the age of twelve to work on his family's Anne Arundel County tobacco farm after his family freed their slaves, he lacked all but a basic formal education. His mother, Hannah, did her best to continue her son's education, and there is some evidence that the local schoolmaster was a frequent dinner guest, where, perhaps in return for a meal, he also helped to further the boy's education. There is no doubt that young Johns had a deep interest in learning and took the initiative himself to supplement his mother's instruction with his own reading.

Urged on by his mother's prophetic advice, "Thee has business ability," Johns left the family homestead at the age of seventeen to work for his uncle in Baltimore. Getting his start in dry goods—including running his uncle's business in the elder's absence during the worst days of the War of 1812—he was involved in trade with settlers to the north and south of Baltimore and as far west as Ohio. Prior to the railroads, the only way to move goods across the Appalachian Mountains was by horse-drawn wagon. Since corn was more easily (and profitably) transported over the mountains in distilled form, this resulted in a lucrative business trading dry goods to settlers in the Ohio River Valley in exchange for barrels of whiskey. Not only was this contrary to the beliefs of the Society of Friends (Quakers), his own uncle deplored Johns's efforts to "sell souls into perdition."

Perhaps selling alcohol against the wishes of his uncle and his church shows a measure of his self-reliance and determination as a young entrepreneur. Against the advice of many, including his elders, he did what he believed was right and also that which would help himself to prosper. It is very likely that his experience with horse-drawn wagons made the new railroads seem much less of a gamble in the 1840s. At a time when other businessmen considered railroads a risky investment, Johns saw their promise and embraced the new technology. Consequently, he became a major early shareholder in the Baltimore & Ohio Railroad, controlling the railroad's purse strings as chairman of the Finance Committee, and backing it with his own fortune during adverse financial situations. Known as a staunch Unionist during the Civil War, Hopkins hosted a dinner in 1863 for Secretary of the Treasury Salmon P. Chase, railroad executives, and local businessmen, where all pledged support for emancipation and assured President Abraham Lincoln that the B&O Railroad would assist the government with moving troops and supplies. Later in his life, having prospered greatly from his various business endeavors, he became a private financier, lending money to individuals and businesses at competitive interest rates. He derived great satisfaction from lending money to young entrepreneurs who had been turned down by banks. He had a keen eye for a person's potential and was rarely wrong in his judgment. When an acquaintance complimented him for doing a good deed in helping a fledgling business get off the ground, he avowed that it was strictly business and had nothing to do with personal feelings. The borrower prospered, and Johns made money as well.

Although generous with family and acquaintances—if they could prove need and the ability to use money wisely—Johns was not known as a philanthropist until very late in his life. So why did he decide to found a university and a hospital? Indirect influences—his family history and Quaker faith—likely played a part. One may only speculate with caution, but several members of the extended Hopkins clan took stands or made proposals that neighbors may have found unusual, or even radical. Quakers were among the first Marylanders to express organized opposition to slavery, for example; Johns's uncle Jarred Hopkins and an uncle by marriage (to his aunt Margaret), Jessie Tyson, took active part in the founding of the first antislavery society in Maryland in 1789. Later, as a member of the House of Delegates in the mid-1820s, Jessie and Margaret's son John Tyson spoke out strongly in favor of extending civil rights to Jews in Maryland. The idea of doing something new, different, or against the grain did not frighten these relatives. More directly, Johns Hopkins, having lived in Baltimore since the age of seventeen, was aware of the poor quality of medical care in the city and so perhaps wished to improve those conditions. While lack of formal education proved no hindrance to success in business, he no doubt regretted his educational deficiencies, so he may have yearned to provide educational opportunities for others.

In any case, Thom does not mention Johns's reason for founding the two institutions. Had he discussed his plans with other family members, such discussions would have been related to Thom by her father, uncles, and aunts, as so many other events were. But this was in keeping with his quiet personality; rather than brag about the great good he intended to achieve for mankind with his fortune, he kept such thoughts to himself as he pondered his mortality and legacy. He was certainly aware of local philanthropists such as Moses Sheppard, a fellow Quaker, and the emphasis of the Society of Friends on assisting those in need. Around 1870, Hopkins himself reportedly donated ten thousand dollars toward the building of a home for the Baltimore chapter of the Young Men's Christian Association.

One man who probably influenced Hopkins to leave his fortune as a major bequest was George Peabody. A contemporary who also made his fortune in business and finance, he founded the Peabody Institute in Baltimore in 1857. While Hopkins's family seems to be silent on the matter (Thom does not mention Peabody), Peabody's biographer claims that George directly influenced Johns to leave his fortune as a lasting legacy. A published account states that John Work Garrett invited Hopkins and Peabody to dinner one evening in 1867. Both Hopkins and Peabody were born in 1795 and both had amassed large fortunes, but Peabody was already known for his cultural and educational philanthropy in Great Britain and the United States. Garrett was a long-time friend and business associate of Hopkins in the B&O Railroad, and he wanted Peabody to urge Hopkins to leave his fortune to education and health care. Peabody, who knew Hopkins only casually, stated that he would not urge Hopkins to do anything, but would only relate his personal experience. The story continues that this dinner took place, Peabody related what he had done with his own fortune, and, two days later, Hopkins announced his intention to found a university and a hospital. Franklin Parker, in *George Peabody: A Biography* (Vanderbilt University Press, 1971), relates the outcome of the meeting in these words: "Hopkins was obviously so carried away by Peabody's personality and his educational interests that he made his will the very next day" (p. 166). Neither Peabody nor Hopkins commented on that momentous evening, but there is reason to doubt this account. While the exact date of this meeting is in doubt, it most likely took place in April 1867; Peabody died in 1869. The date on the copy of Hopkins's will that was presented to the court is July 9, 1870. There is no mention of the executed will (including two later codicils) superseding a previous will.

Other circumstantial evidence argues against Parker's account. Hopkins was known for deliberation in making major financial decisions. He certainly took risks, but only after examining the benefits and drawbacks of a proposed course of action, so it is difficult to believe that Peabody could have persuaded Hopkins so convincingly in one evening that Hopkins would announce his plans immediately afterward. It seems likely that Hopkins was already thinking of his legacy, and perhaps was already considering founding an educational institution. He could have chosen the easier path and left his money to an existing institution, any one of which would have been delirious at the prospect of adding seven million dollars to its coffers. With no wife or direct descendants, he was free to distribute his fortune as he pleased. Johns was aware of Peabody's beneficence and the latter's actions very likely influenced his thinking. Perhaps Peabody provided the final arguments, or helped Hopkins firm up his plans to found two new institutions rather than donating to existing universities or hospitals.

Regardless of Peabody's influence, on August 24, 1867, after receiving formal approval from the Maryland legislature, Johns Hopkins published a "Certificate of Incorporation," signed by his hand-picked trustees. This document serves as the charter for the Johns Hopkins University. Of the original twelve-member university Board of Trustees, two trustees were blood relatives: William Hopkins was a cousin and Lewis N. Hopkins a nephew. Two other relatives by marriage, Richard M. Janney and Francis White, were also named to the board. White was also one of the executors of Hopkins's will. Six of the original twelve trustees were Quakers, and all of the non-relatives were acquaintances through various business endeavors. One of his hand-picked trustees, John Fonerden, died in 1869 and was replaced by James Carey Thomas when the trustees met for the first time in 1870. On the same occasion in 1867, Hopkins incorporated the Johns Hopkins Hospital, also naming a twelve-member Board of Trustees, with ten members serving on both boards.

Just over six years after the formal incorporation, Johns Hopkins passed away on Christmas Eve 1873. In 1874, his bequest became a reality, and the trustees could begin planning in earnest. Hopkins left detailed instructions for the establishment of the hospital, including its location and stipulations on who it should serve, but he mentioned the university in just one paragraph. He preferred that the university be located on the grounds of his Clifton estate, but—perhaps in keeping with his plain lifestyle—he intended that his bequest serve as an endowment and not be used to build magnificent structures. Founding president Daniel Coit Gilman later paraphrased Hopkins's desire as "Build men, not buildings." To carry out this wish, the trustees ultimately decided to build in downtown Baltimore, a few blocks west of the Mount Vernon district, with the intention that the university eventually would move to Clifton.

Hopkins had no experience with higher education, so perhaps his lack of precise wording meant that he did not presume to dictate what form the university should take. The problem was, none of his trustees were educators, so they, too, had no idea what the university should be. Casting about for help, the trustees contacted the presidents of several established institutions, soliciting their advice. Charles Eliot of Harvard, Andrew White of Cornell, and James Angell of the University of Michigan were very generous with their assistance. While they differed on many points, all three advised the trustees to find a president—someone with experience running a university—and delegate to him all but the highest-level decisions. Upon inquiry, the name mentioned most frequently was that of Daniel Coit Gilman. Fortuitously, Gilman was eager to leave the University of California, where he had served as president for two years, to return east, and he accepted the presidency in early 1875. Gilman believed that the infant university offered a rare chance to start from scratch and do something completely different. The result of Gilman's labors was an emphasis on research, not just by faculty, but by graduate and undergraduate students, modeled on the German approach to university education that had spread throughout Europe. This method, adopted by nearly all American colleges and universities by the late 1800s, is embodied in the concept of the seminar, where students perform original research, present the results in class, and then have their work critiqued by their instructor and peers. From this new idea grew a center for research and teaching that soon became known around the world.

One notes two errors in Thom's original work, both on page 73. Near the top she states, "Nine of the twelve directors were to sit on the boards of both institutions." The two boards in fact shared ten common members. Farther down that page, she reports, "The University was inaugurated February 22, 1876 by an address delivered in the Academy of Music by Thomas Huxley." Here, Thom has confused two separate events. February 22 became known as Commemoration Day because that was when Gilman was formally inaugurated as the first president in 1876. Charles Eliot of Harvard spoke, and Gilman also delivered his Inaugural Address. Huxley was not present on that occasion. He was present on September 12, 1876, at which time he delivered his (in)famous address, "University Education."

For further study on the history of the Johns Hopkins University, two books are indispensable. John C. French wrote *A History of the University Founded by Johns Hopkins*, published by the then-named Johns Hopkins Press in 1946. This is a fairly complete history of the first seventy years. In 1960, Hugh Hawkins completed a dissertation, "Pioneer: A History of the Johns Hopkins University, 1874–1889." Originally published by the Cornell University Press, and now available again through the Johns Hopkins University Press, this is a scholarly account of the founding of the university and its earliest years. Both books include in their early pages sketches of the founder. Although not a traditional chronological history, Mame Warren's *Johns Hopkins: Knowledge for the World*, published by the Johns Hopkins University in 2000, offers perceptive insights on the university's history, built around Gilman's inaugural address.

For an excellent biographical sketch of Johns Hopkins, see Kathryn Allamong Jacob's "Mr. Johns Hopkins" in the January 1974 issue of the *Johns Hopkins Magazine*. This article is also available on the Web at www.library.jhu.edu/collections/specialcollections/archives/jacob.html. An earlier illustrated biographical essay also appeared in the *Johns Hopkins Magazine*: Anthony Neville and Joanne Delp wrote "A Portrait of the Man: Johns Hopkins" in February 1963. The extensive Papers of George Peabody are in the holdings of the Peabody Essex Museum, Salem, Massachusetts.

JAMES STIMPERT
Archivist, Sheridan Libraries
The Johns Hopkins University

INTRODUCTION

THE justification for a biography of Johns Hopkins is twofold. In any account of the beginnings of higher education in America he has a significance inseparable from that of the two foundations which bear his name; and in the economic history of his own city his was a dominant figure in a period of high interest and in activities of supreme importance for its future prosperity. It is difficult for any man of great wealth to be correctly estimated by his own generation; and since few knew or comprehended the vision which Johns Hopkins cherished and the purposes for which he destined his millions, he was more than usually misunderstood. It is fitting that the story of his life should be told now—at a time when the lapse of more than half a century has given us perspective and when, nevertheless, the image of his stooped but masterful figure lingers in the memory of persons yet living.

The materials for a life of Johns Hopkins are necessarily scanty. He was a merchant and a banker, not a man of public affairs, nor in any sense a man of letters. He left, therefore, no voluminous journal, no public speeches, no literary letters composed with a consciousness that posterity was looking over his shoulder. It is only by a fortunate chance that the story of his apprenticeship in his uncle's store and of the circumstances which first gave loose rein to his genius for business has been preserved in reminiscences which he gave to a relative. For an adequate account of the influence of Johns Hopkins on the financial history of Baltimore—his part in protecting the credit of the city in panics and his farsighted encouragement of new projects—the sources are yet wanting and must wait upon further research.

To the writing of a biography of Johns Hopkins the author of the present work brings the interest of kinship and personal recollection as well as a lifelong loyalty to the institutions which he founded. Her effort has been not merely to preserve the meager records, but to answer the natural question, What manner of man was he? by presenting the very human figure of that quiet Quaker merchant who chanced to have an unusual genius for judging men and foreseeing business trends, and who kept through a long life ideals that finally flowered in one of the most notable of American benefactions.

JOHN C. FRENCH
Librarian, The Johns Hopkins University

September 16, 1929

FOREWORD

I HAVE always had a latent desire to record the personal characteristics of my great-uncle, Johns Hopkins, and to tell the main events in his life. This persistent ambition is an illustration of the way in which a small and apparently insignificant act in one's life leads on to more far-reaching things; for once when I was a very little girl, I peeped into the big dining-room at Clifton and there found Uncle Johns sitting alone at the end of the long dining-table. All the guests had left the room and he was about to do so. Seeing me timidly looking about, he beckoned me to him, put me on his knee, and gave me a taste of his champagne. I liked it very much and I wanted some more, but my father came in at that moment and remonstrated.

"Oh, let the child have it," said great-uncle Johns in a hearty manner; and he continued giving me tastes until I was taken off to bed. Perhaps he was wrong, but his understanding ways formed a bond between us which has lasted ever since. Somehow I felt that he was on my side and that, in some indefinable way, I knew him better than did the grown-ups. Later on I felt sincere regret when I learned that Uncle Johns had asked my parents to come and live with him and that they had not been willing to accept.

I hope, therefore, that in this brief outline of his life I may put Johns Hopkins before its readers in his true light and give information upon a character so little known and so richly deserving of admiration and esteem.

ILLUSTRATIONS

CHAPTER ONE

THE EARLY LIFE OF JOHNS HOPKINS

THE man who has colored the thought of the modern world, through the influence of two notable institutions which bear his name, The Johns Hopkins University and The Johns Hopkins Hospital, was born in the year 1795 on a tobacco plantation in Anne Arundel county, Maryland, half way between Baltimore and Annapolis.

The infant nation which claimed Johns Hopkins as a son of her soil was at this time scarcely of age, lacking two years of being twenty-one. George Washington still held it by the hand and it was rapidly learning to walk alone. Though the recent vigorous use of its fists had shown Mother England its mettle, this youthful country still clung to English lore and tradition. Its counties and towns and its private estates bore witness by their names to their English parentage, and "Whitehall," the birthplace of Johns Hopkins, was in this respect no exception. It was owned by Samuel Hopkins, his father, and was part of a tract of land granted by the King to one William Hopkins.

Five hundred acres of long green tobacco plants formed the background for the unpretentious brick house, the large barns, and the slaves' quarters, a group of log cabins, usually surrounded by pickaninnies and old mammies while the more able-bodied negroes were busy in the fields.

1

Though "Whitehall' was a house of only moderate size, yet here, in the early days, were entertained many parties of friends and relatives from North Carolina and the Valley of Virginia, for the Hopkins family were sociable people and the latch-string was always out. These visitors traveled on horse-back, bringing what baggage they could strapped to the backs of the saddles and following the Indian trails. The ample barns and stables of "Whitehall" easily accommodated the extra horses and hospitality was always to be counted on.

In this land of sand and sunshine, of frequent streams and rolling country, fox-hunting was the chief diversion; and for generations there had been a pack of hounds and plenty of riding horses in the Hopkins family. Many a morning at "sun-up" Johns and his older brother, Joseph, would saddle "Tom" and "Rattler," and calling the hounds gallop over the fields of sedge.

These were days of ease and plenty. Johns Hopkins's father, Samuel Hopkins, had bought out the shares of his brothers in the plantation, and had thus become the sole owner of a large tract of land lying between the Severn River and the Magothy. He had married Hannah Janney, of Loudon County, Virginia, whose family were people of means and prominence. It was in 1792 that Samuel, then a man of thirty-three years, had brought his bride from the Valley of Virginia to be the mistress of "Whitehall;" and in this maid of eighteen were latent those truly great qualities of motherhood which once prompted the statement that

"Whitehall," the Birthplace of Johns Hopkins Near Millersville, Anne Arundel County, Maryland

there never was a great man the elements of whose greatness might not be traced to the original characteristics and early influence of his mother. She was a woman of spirit, fortitude, and high ideals; and she and Samuel both took a prominent part in the Society of Friends, to which they belonged.

The Hopkins family had not always been Friends; they were of English stock and had belonged to the Church of England; but when in 1671, George Fox, the great Quaker preacher, visited the colonies and spread the doctrine of Friends, he converted many to his religion and among others Gerard (or Garrard) Hopkins, styled "Gentleman," the great-grandfather of Johns. This Gerard, a man of some note, and one of a committee appointed in 1732 to welcome Lord Baltimore, married Margaret Johns, daughter of Richard Johns, the owner of an estate of some four thousand acres of land in Calvert County, Maryland. Richard Johns was spoken of as "a man of good credit and repute;" and it was from this ancestor, his great-great-grandfather, that Johns Hopkins received his Christian name. The old estate of the Johns family was known as "The Clifts," and it is notable that Johns Hopkins named his country seat "Clifton" in memory of the home of his ancestors in Calvert County.

To Samuel and Hannah Hopkins were born eleven children, six sons, of whom Johns was the second, and five daughters. They had ample means to meet their simple needs, and plenty of faithful slaves to care for the children and attend to the duties of their large household; and the years of plenty rolled peacefully around.

On "First Day" (Sunday) the family rode or drove to the West River Meeting-House, where they sat, the women and girls on one side, the men and boys on the other. Now and then Hannah would rise and in her soft voice make a prayer or deliver a sermon with dignity and quiet force. Johns often thought of his mother in after years as she stood in Meeting; her sweet face and womanly presence made a picture which he never forgot. Samuel was a popular man in the neighborhood and prominent in the Society of Friends. He was an Elder and Overseer in the West River Meeting, and in 1808 he was appointed one of a committee to select a site for the first Quaker Meeting-House in the city of Washington. He was an affectionate father, a devoted husband, and a man of high principles. He and Hannah with their eleven children were an unusually happy and united family.

Until Johns Hopkins was about twelve years old there seemed no cloud to darken the horizon. Tobacco was a profitable crop and found a ready market in England. Such was the demand for it that English agents were placed at all the river ports to secure the crops and prevent their being diverted to France and to Holland. Through his Tobacco Plantations Samuel Hopkins had become a man of ample means.

During the first few years of that century which was destined to bring freedom to the civilized world, a new note began to be sounded among the Friends. On

Sundays, after meetings, little animated groups would form on the lawn of the Meeting-House to discuss a tremendous and devastating change which was being contemplated. "Abolition" was a political question which had begun to stir the country; but for the Quakers it had become a question of principle. Whether the country decided to free the slaves or not, there was still a right and a wrong in the matter, and this must be settled by them to the satisfaction of their own consciences no matter what the political outcome might be.

We can picture the anguish of spirit with which that little band of Quakers in Anne Arundel faced this tremendous question. Free the slaves? Terrible would be the consequences of such an act! Boys taken from school to work on the plantations! Hard physical labor for entire families accustomed to ease and leisure! To manumit the slaves in whom large sums of money had been invested, and let them go without compensation—that way lay Ruin!

It was a hard and a perplexing time and mental anguish preceded decision. For months Samuel and Hannah could think of nothing else. All of the work of the plantation, as well as of the household was done by the slaves. The cloth for the boys' and men's suits was woven on the place, and even some of the hats were made by slave labor. Who would till the fields and harvest the crops when the slaves were gone? Who would card the wool and the cotton, do the weaving in the weaving-house, and keep the spinning wheels humming with the gentle burr that daily filled the air?

Samuel Hopkins had been a good master to his slaves; he had fed them well and clothed them well. Once every year he would measure them all for shoes, notching peach-sticks to correspond to the length of the many feet, and then gathering these into bundles, he would go to the city and buy shoes and clothing of various kinds, enough to last a year. He had been kind and considerate to those who served him, and now was he to be plunged into poverty by turning them all loose on the world to look out for themselves? It was almost as dark an outlook for the slaves as for their masters. The young and old were helpless and entirely dependent. They would have to stay and be cared for though they made little return in labor.

There was "Aunt Minty," the well-beloved Mammy. Could they part with her? And there was her mother, a very old woman, who had come over from Africa years before, bringing with her a lump of Guinea gold which she had given to her mistress, Hannah, and which had been made into cuff-buttons for Joseph, the oldest son, and engraved with his initials.

There were many perplexing sides of the question to be faced. Abolition was very unpopular in the neighborhood among those who were not Quakers, many of whom were dear friends of Samuel and Hannah. How would they feel toward those who voluntarily freed their slaves?

The time came at last for a final decision and the

Society of Friends took a firm stand. All were to set free their slaves without compensation of any sort or be put out of Meeting.

Samuel Hopkins paced the floor for three nights trying to adjust his mind to the changes that would come if he obeyed this ultimatum. Hannah stood by advising and encouraging him. They knew that if they took this momentous step it meant robbing their children of their full share of education. It meant great responsibility for themselves, self-denial, and added burdens; and it meant very careful economy to make it possible to keep the plantation.

At last a decision was reached and the life of the Hopkins family turned a corner. Because of something unexplainable, but perhaps divine, which manifests itself now and then in men and women, Samuel and Hannah were able, though blood and sweat were the price, to lift their eyes unto the hills and see the vision. And so all of the able-bodied negroes belonging to Samuel Hopkins were set free in the year 1807. Those who still needed care and protection were kept. A cabin was given to Aunt Minty's old mother to occupy for the rest of her life, and an allowance of sixty dollars a year, a sum which was considered ample in those days.

The memory of these early days was always a vivid picture in the mind of Johns Hopkins. He had an intense admiration for his father and mother, and he and his sisters and brothers were brought into closer sympathy than is usual by conditions which obliged them to help each other in many ways. Johns was

often the care-taker for the younger ones. The South
River School was a mile distant from Whitehall and
necessitated a long walk twice a day for the children
of the Hopkins family. Joseph, the oldest, being away
at school in Alexandria, it fell to Johns to see that his
younger sisters and brothers reached the school and
returned safely and in good order each day. Having
been their care-taker in youth, through life he assumed
a protectorate over them, and when his brother Joseph
died in 1845, leaving four young sons, Johns was named
as their guardian.

After the momentous decision to free their slaves,
came the end of the golden days for Samuel Hopkins
and his family. Joseph, the oldest son, was called home
from school. Labor and anxiety took the place of the
happy companionship of classmates. Samuel, though
no longer a young man, had to rise early and work hard
to superintend and direct the activities of the large
plantation. Things had to be kept going with the help
of the young negro boys and girls and those who, though
old, could still work a little. Samuel's own son,
Joseph, had to put his shoulder to the wheel, and Johns,
though only a boy of twelve, was kept busy on the
plantation helping in such ways as he could.

Hannah's evenings were not times of leisure; but not
for a moment did she allow the cares and worries and
the daily drag of a large family to blind her spiritual
vision. Instead of complaining of her changed life
or becoming depressed, when the winter evenings were
only the uneventful endings of long days of unaccus-

tomed labor, she read from the fine old literature available to her and was refreshed and uplifted by such intellectual contact. With her spinning wheel in front of her and a book propped up on a conveniently arranged shelf, she managed to spin and at the same time to read aloud to her children. She was thoroughly conversant with the classics, and her favorite book was The Iliad of Homer, with which she finally became so familiar that she was able to recite it from beginning to end. Her children also memorized large portions of it. She was a rock of strength to her husband and an inspiration to her children. No wonder that the boy Johns through all his life was so devoted to his mother, and that one of his greatest pleasures later on was to be able to give her the leisure and luxury she so richly deserved. It was in these early days that habits of strict economy as well as principles of integrity were grounded in him by the example of his parents and especially by the unselfish devotion of his mother.

During the War of 1812, when all communication with England was cut off and no goods could be purchased from abroad, Hannah Hopkins knitted suits for her children. Wool from her sheep was carded, dyed, and spun under her own personal supervision. When communication was again opened, one of her sons was sent to Annapolis to make much needed purchases, and a gentleman seeing the boy in his knitted suit exclaimed, "That boy must have a good mother!"

Johns was intensely interested in his studies, and the love of learning was encouraged not only by his mother

but also by the master of the South River school, which
he had attended. This man was an Oxford graduate,
a highly educated gentleman, and a lover of books and
literature. Under him Johns formed a taste for reading which lasted all his life, and though he was obliged
to leave school so early as he did, he became, with the
aid of his good memory, a remarkably well read man.

South River school was a branch of King William's
school in Annapolis, the first Free School established
in America. In 1696 a petition for a free school in
Maryland had been addressed to his Most Excellent
Majesty, King William. "The act explained the needs
of the Province for the establishment of free schools
and asked the royal permission for such a school in
Anne-Arundel-Town, upon the Severn River, to be
named after the King and to be under the special
guidance of the Archbishop of Canterbury. The Royal
permission was obtained, and certain lots of land in
Annapolis, together with the "Kentish House," an
ample brick building still standing in the shadow of the
State House, were given for this school. Its purpose
was, "to prepare both English and Indian boys for his
Majesty's Royal College of William and Mary, in
Virginia" and for the "propagation of the Gospel and
the education of the youth of the Province in good
letters and manners."

The school was finally conveyed, with its property,
funds, masters, and students to St. John's College in
Annapolis, whose beautiful colonial buildings still greet
the visitor entering this quaint old town.

The success of King William's school led to an extension of the free school system in other parts of Maryland; and in 1723 free schools were located in the twelve Counties of the Province. It was that branch, or extension, of King William's school at the head of South River which Johns Hopkins attended, and to which his young brother, Gerard, became what was called a "visitor," in 1823. Gerard is spoken of as a "Planter whose home lay among the hills but a mile from the school building." He must have been a remarkable boy, for at this time he seems to have been not more than sixteen years of age. The visitors to these free schools were chosen from among the best men of the counties, and were conscientious in maintaining a high standard. When chosen for the position of visitor, each man had to serve the public in this capacity or forfeit one hundred pounds of tobacco. The influence of Gerard Hopkins was immediately felt. He advocated abandoning free scholarships, substituting the paying of a small tuition fee for each pupil, and urged the using of such fees for improvements upon the school lands and buildings. These suggestions were adopted.

The South River school was built on a tract of 150 acres of land "purchased from Mr. Richard Snowden" and known as "God Wills" and "Iron Mine." The building was of two stories, seventeen by twenty-five feet. The first story consisted of one large schoolroom with a great fireplace. Two rooms upstairs, with a fireplace in each, constituted the residence of the Master. The Masters were required to be: "of the Church of England and of pious and exemplary lives and conversations and capable of teaching well, Grammar, good writing and the Mathematicks, if such could conveniently be got at twenty pounds sterling ($100) a year and the free use of the school plantation."

Such, however, could not often "be got," and most of the schools suffered in consequence. South River school, however, was most fortunate in this respect. The great prosperity of the colony brought many Englishmen of education to Maryland in search of their fortunes. They often met the fate of most adventurers and were quite frequently obliged to resort to teaching. This master at South River was no doubt one of these.

Among the group of country boys who filled up the main room of that little South River school, the master soon came to look for "Johnsie Hopkins," a blue-eyed, long-legged boy whose eager, intelligent face showed the deep interest he felt in his studies. Johns loved History and English Literature, and it was his delight to recite long passages from his favorite poems.

The time came, however, when he was sorely needed on the farm, and when he must put his shoulder to the wheel as his brother Joseph had done. School must be given up. No more meeting with the other boys at the cross-roads in the early morning; no more friendly days in the school-yard; no more loitering along the road with school-mates in the long afternoons. Stern necessity beckoned and the boy had to take on the ways of the man.

It was arranged that Johns should study his lessons at home from time to time through the day, as he was able, and on Saturday evenings the Master of the School came to dine with the Hopkins family and heard Johns recite his lessons. The whole family looked forward to this as the most delightful part of the week. The schoolmaster was a very interesting man, who would stay and talk after the lessons were over. It is partly to the inspiration of this English man of letters that we may attribute the later founding of the famous seat of learning in Baltimore. He implanted a love of learning which, thwarted in Johns Hopkins's early years, found compensation later in giving to others that for which he himself had longed.

In the hard school of necessity the young Johns Hopkins was shaped into habits of self-denial, industry, and thrift. This early training, added to his natural ability, fitted him when opportunity offered later on, not only to assume the responsibilities of a man of wealth, but also to occupy many positions of trust. In later life he used the great fortune which he had accumulated to help youths who were anxious as he had been for a wider education.

CHAPTER TWO

WHEN Johns Hopkins was seventeen years old, his mother told him he must not stay any longer on the plantation. "Thee has business ability," she said, "and thee must go where the money is." Accordingly his father's brother, Gerard Hopkins, took him into his wholesale grocery business, and leaving the old homestead he went to live in Baltimore with his Uncle's family.

He is said to have arrived at his Uncle's house with a valise containing a very modest supply of clothing and a large bag of "Aunt Minty's" ginger cakes. He soon became fast friends with his young cousins there and especially with their mother, whom he called "Aunt Dolly." Tradition says that they both had a keen sense of humor and that she frequently shielded him from the strict discipline of his Uncle. One of the rules which Johns was expected to obey obliged him to be in bed by nine o'clock, and frequently at the breakfast table Gerard would inquire at what hour Johns had come in. With a wink at his Aunt Dolly he would reply "I believe it was a little after nine, wasn't it, Aunt Dolly?" and she would reply, "Yes, Johns, it was a little after nine," both carefully failing to mention the exact hour.

To his favorite cousin, Thomas Hopkins, Johns Hopkins gave the following account of this part of his

14

Mrs. Gerard Hopkins, "Aunt Dolly"
From painting in possession of Mrs. Nathaniel Crenshaw

life: "When I was a boy, thy father having come to
South River to visit my parents, noticing I was an
active boy on the farm, he asked my Mother to let me
come to live with him and he would bring me up a
Merchant. At the age of seventeen I came and stayed
in my Uncle's store. He was a wholesale Grocery and
Commission Merchant and I lived in his family. He
was very kind to me and his wife was like a mother.
She was always pleasant and cheerful and anxious to
promote my happiness in every way. I was very fond
of my Uncle and Aunt and contented and happy
with them.

"My Uncle was a Minister in the Society of Friends,
and his company was much sought after. He trans-
acted a large business, was always cheerful, and often
indulged in anecdotes and innocent mirth. When I
was but nineteen years of age, my Uncle was appointed
by the Baltimore Yearly Meeting of Friends to go out
to the State of Ohio to attend the opening of the First
Yearly Meeting of Friends to be held in Mount Pleasant. My Aunt's health being delicate at that time,
she accompanied him, and with three others, a party of
five in all, they set out on their, at that time, long and
perilous journey. They all travelled on horseback,
and a great part of their way led through a wilderness
country with no safe roads, only the Indian paths to
travel and many rivers to ford. It was thought to be
a great undertaking, but they performed the long
journey and returned after an absence of several
months in safety and in good health.

"Previous to my Uncle's leaving, he arranged his business affairs. He then called me to him and said: 'I am going this long journey and thee is but a youth; now I want thee to put an old head on young shoulders; as thee has been faithful to my interests since thee has been with me, I am going to leave everything in thy hands. Here are checks which I have signed my name to; they are upwards of five hundred, Thee can deposit the money as it is received in bank; and as thee wants money, thee can fill out these checks which I leave with thee. Buy goods, and do the best thee can. Be attentive to the house and see after the little children, whom we leave behind in thy care and that of a female relative!

"So we shook hands and parted. I felt my responsibility to be very great, did as my Uncle told me, and on his return, on looking over his affairs, he was surprised to find I had done much better than he had expected. I had increased his business considerably, and it is with pride and pleasure that I look back to that time and to the great confidence my Uncle reposed in me.

"I had to undergo much anxiety during their absence. It was in the year 1814; the British forces had entered Washington, burned the capitol, and all kinds of rumors reached me. I well knew they would come to Baltimore. At last the unwelcome news was brought us; they were coming up the Chesapeake.

"The citizens were alarmed, many leaving the city, and great confusion prevailed. I, having charge of the store and seeing after the little children at the dwelling and the relative who attended to them, it seemed to me that I had to carry a great load. I felt it my duty to stay at the store, but the children would have to be sent away. While I was troubled and debating in my own mind what I should do, and where to send the children, as the people were fleeing in every direction, to my great surprise and joy my Uncle and Aunt arrived home, three days before the bombardment of Fort McHenry and the Battle of North Point."

The timely arrival of his Aunt and Uncle was indeed most fortunate, for the eventful period which followed affected the whole country, and the disturbance centered around Baltimore. A writer of Baltimore's history says: "the audacity and the appalling success of the American ships and their Commanders in their own waters was such a turning of the tables that . . . . the whole venom of the modern Goths seemed concentrated against the Baltimoreans."

Baltimore was not only the greatest tobacco shipping port of this part of the world but was also an important port for the shipping of grain and flour to the West Indies. There was also a large trade between this port and the West Indies in sugar and much importation of coffee from South America. Many of the sailing vessels carrying on this extensive commerce were converted into privateers, and more of such vessels sailed from the port of Baltimore than from Philadelphia, New York, or Boston.

On September 9 the British Fleet sailed up the Bay

and on the eleventh anchored off North Point. "Nelson's marines, victors of the Battle of the Nile and Trafalgar; Wellington's Invincibles, fresh from the conquest of Napoleon and the Peninsular Campaign, had no forebodings." The battle which raged through the night was a terrific bombardment and struck terror to the listeners, uncertain of the city's fate. Francis Scott Key, pacing the deck of the "Minden" beheld by the morning's light the great folds of the American flag still floating from Fort McHenry in the harbor of Baltimore and wrote the inspired words of the "Star Spangled Banner," our National Anthem.

"It was not Saratoga nor Yorktown which struck the mortal blows to England's supremacy; she could afford to lose a few thousand mercenary Hessians, but the loss of her maritime ascendency touched her to the quick . . . . American freedom and equality upon the seas was achieved by the victories of the cruisers and privateers; and in this Baltimore and the fast clipper ships of the Chesapeake played a vastly more potential part than any other section of the country."

The Baltimore to which Johns Hopkins had come as a boy of seventeen was very different from the great city of to-day. A few stately mansions dotted the surrounding hills, while the town itself built close to its landlocked harbor, was only a few years old, having been granted its Charter as a city in 1796. There were no tall structures, and few public buildings of any sort, and the streets were paved with cobble-stones. No railroads puffed their smoke into the city's lungs,

A CLIPPER SHIP

By courtesy of the Baltimore "Sun"

no poles or wires gave suggestion of that great sleeping
giant, electricity, which lay undiscovered; and even
steam was in its early infancy and gave little promise of
the wonders to be. The tall masts of the great clipper
ships towered above the wharves, and the straggling
streets, lined with low houses, mostly of frame, seemed
centered at the foot of the hills and close to the water.
No honk of machine or clang of trolley disturbed the
quiet—a seaboard town lapped by the waves, in the
hush that preceded the birth of modern industry.

A giant flag floated from Fort McHenry, its stars
and stripes, new-born and self-conscious, flaunting
defiance in the face of the English vessels at anchor
loading their cargoes of tobacco. Covered Conestoga
wagons, spattered with mud, crowded in from the
West, forming long lines down the main streets, their
blue-shirted teamsters gathering for refreshments at
the numerous inns.

Here, in its sheltered harbor, where the Patapsco
stretched out into the Bay, lay the promise, for such
as could read it, of a great commercial city to be.
Grain came in from the West, tobacco from the alluvial
soil of Anne Arundel County; truck and produce from
the Eastern Shore, and fish, oysters, and crabs from
the Chesapeake.

Commercially, Baltimore was, from its earliest days,
destined to take a leading part and to become a great
shipping and manufacturing center; but let it not be
forgotten that it is to the clear vision and liberality of a
few of her early citizens that she owes her position

to-day as a seat of art and of learning, as well as of commercial supremacy. She has taken her place among the great intellectual centers because of the generosity and public spirit of such men as Johns Hopkins, George Peabody, and Enoch Pratt.

Prior to 1812 and the Embargo, which prevented all goods from being shipped out of this country, there had been great commercial activity. The deadening effects of the Revolutionary War had largely disappeared, while the war between France and England had interfered with the commerce of those countries and had thrown much of it to the ships of the States, and especially to the fast clipper ships of the Chesapeake.

In three years after it had become a city Baltimore had grown to be third in size in the Union, with a social and commercial prestige which had formerly centered at Annapolis, when that town had been the home of the Proprietary Governor and the Royal Collector. Its social prominence had been emphasized by the visit of Jerome Bonaparte and his marriage to the beautiful Betsy Patterson, and also by the fact that being at a convenient distance between Washington and Philadelphia, General Washington often made it his stopping-place when journeying to the latter city. He had said, indeed; "Baltimore is the risingest town in America, except the Federal City [Washington]." Already the beautiful homes of some of the wealthier Baltimoreans had been built; "Hampden," "Belvedere," "Bolton;" and in 1800 "Homewood," built by Charles Carroll, thrilled the community by such beautiful symmetry and graceful proportions that it may well serve now as the key-note in the architectural scheme of the Johns Hopkins University.

While Johns Hopkins was establishing himself in the business world of Baltimore, his parents were meeting the unusual exigencies of the Embargo by storing up the crops of tobacco which they were unable to export. Samuel and his wife, Hannah, with the help and advice of their oldest son, Joseph, built large barns to store their tobacco in until the Embargo should be lifted. After three years their crops were sold for what was then the large sum of ten thousand dollars. Samuel, however, did not live to see the fruits of his forethought. His health failed, and he died February 9, 1814. His niece, Sarah Hopkins, writes of him,

"He was an upright, noble-minded man, polite, considerate, and entertaining in conversation, and much beloved by his friends and acquaintances. He was useful in society, his neighborhood, and family. As he drew near his final close, his virtues shone more brightly. What strength of mind, what patience, what fortitude; his mind was firm and unshaken as a rock and his last words were, 'All is well.' "

As someone has well said, this in itself is a heritage.

CHAPTER THREE

ELIZABETH

JOHNS HOPKINS lived for seven years in his uncle Gerard's family. During this period he developed into a tall and unusually strong man. He was handsome, though his large features and firm mouth betokened strength rather than beauty and formed an appropriate setting for his commanding personality. In his manners he was direct, terse, and convincing; and when once he made up his mind, he was not to be easily diverted. His intimate friend and cousin, Thomas Hopkins, says of him:

"He was a close observer of human nature, much of a reader, kept up with the literature of the day, an eminent merchant (later) and genial companion, fond of anecdotes and possessed of general information."

It was at this time, in his early manhood, that there developed the only love in the life of Johns Hopkins. Though he had many "affairs" in later life and was always a loyal champion and an admirer of women, he was known to have loved but one woman sufficiently to ask her to become his wife.

Elizabeth, daughter of his uncle Gerard, who was hardly more than a child when her cousin came to Baltimore, had grown to be a very pretty young woman with more than ordinary attractiveness. Living in the same house for seven years she had learned to care a great deal for her tall, blue-eyed cousin. She saw how her father depended upon him, and she noticed his sympathy with children, his fondness for dogs, his courteous ways toward women, his love of fun and harmless pleasure, and above all, his strong, compelling masculinity. What had been a youthful attachment grew gradually into a devoted love between these two, and they planned to be married.

Things might have come to a happy conclusion for the young lovers, but the prejudice against the marriage of first cousins was especially strong among Friends, and when Gerard Hopkins was told of this engagement he positively forbade it to continue. This unhesitating decision on his part was a shock to Johns and Elizabeth, for it had not occurred to them that their cousinship would be such a serious obstacle to their marriage. They had, it is true, anticipated some opposition, and were prepared to meet it; but all of the young man's attempts to change his uncle's mind were unsuccessful.

Gerard Hopkins remained obdurate and Johns became indignant against what he considered an unwarranted attitude and an opinion not borne out by his own observation of facts. He felt wronged. If his Uncle Gerard was so positive in his convictions, why had he allowed these two young people, at an age when love was forever beckoning, to be thrown so intimately together? He must have seen their attachment growing, must have read the signs. Right under his nose he had allowed things to go on without remonstrance; and now, at the eleventh hour, he had taken

it into his head to object. Some one must have been
talking to his uncle, Johns thought; he wondered why
people couldn't mind their own business.

There was an unpleasant interview between Gerard
Hopkins and his nephew in which Johns expressed
himself forcibly. The older man, seeing the trouble he
was unwillingly causing, was deeply grieved. He had
not realized the nature of the attachment between
these two; he had been blind, he felt, and he blamed
himself. In the light of this new revelation he now
saw the real drift of many little incidents which had
before escaped him and his kind heart, and he felt
keenly his own lack of insight. To him his duty was
clear, however, and firmly he told Elizabeth where he
felt the right course lay. She cried herself to sleep
that night while Johns paced the streets trying to quiet
the storm that raged in his heart.

Feeling it quite impossible to remain under his
uncle's roof, he packed up his things and went to
temporary lodgings elsewhere. For several days he
avoided his uncle's house, debating meantime what
to do.

"First Day" came and he walked alone to the Meeting House. As he drew near, he saw the broad-
brimmed hats of the men and the women's plain, gray
silk bonnets gathering in front of the buliding. It
was too early, he thought, to go in; better to wait
until he would not be obliged to engage in undesired
conversation.

At last, seeing that the familiar figures had all dis-

appeared inside, he walked up to the unadorned brick
building, entered, and stood within the vestibule.
Here two plain doors denoted the entrance for men on
the left and for women on the right. He walked in and
took a back seat. Immediately, however, his eyes
wandered to the other side. There sat Elizabeth a
little further to the front and his heart went out to her.
His uncle Gerard sat along with the Elders on seats
raised up somewhat higher than the congregation and
facing them—a row of dignified figures, men and
women, whose peaceful faces and simple gray costumes
suited the intense quiet. An atmosphere of restfulness
and peace pervaded the place, bidding all petty human
emotions to subside, while something seemed to say,
"Be still and know that *here* is God." In the long-
continued silence Johns Hopkins, looking now and then
at his uncle's face, experienced a revulsion of feeling.
This man, who had been kind and affectionate to him
during all these years; who had brought him to Baltimore
when he was only a youth and had given him his start
in life, looked weary and haggard. Evidently he too
had suffered. On the other side, also among the
Elders, sat his Aunt Dolly, her sweet face wearing an
unfamiliar and troubled expression.

It came over the young man that his own suffering
and interests were not greater than those of these two,
so devoted to Elizabeth and so kind to him. Words
came into his mind without any will on his part and
repeated themselves over and over until he wished
some one would speak or pray and break the monotony.

At last one of the Friends, on the seats facing the congregation, removed his hat, laid it carefully on the seat beside him, slowly arose, and spoke.

In fervent words he impressed upon his listeners the value of sacrifice, of giving up personal interests for the greater good of all. He hoped that Friends realized that no lasting happiness could come from selfish motives, that whenever anyone made a sacrifice in the interests of duty he would find a peace greater than that which the gratification of personal interests could possibly bring. He himself had had a struggle; he had prayed for light and guidance, and the familiar words had come to him as an answer, "He that loseth his life shall find it." He felt that the words might help others; that they had been sent not for him alone but for all.

His message was brief; and presently, replacing his broad-brimmed hat, he took his seat. Again the silence. Some one made a short prayer. Finally two friends on the Elders' seat shook hands and the meeting was over.

The men and women were again mingling and walking home in little family groups. Johns waited till Elizabeth came out, and joining her, asked her to walk with him. They talked of the matter nearest their hearts. Johns pleaded his case as only a man of strong convictions and great personal force can. He told Elizabeth that in her hands lay the making or the marring of their lives; that the love which had grown between them for seven years was not a little thing to be easily cast aside or to be influenced by the prejudices of other people; that it was something which would endure the strain of time, something so much a part of their lives that nothing else would ever compare to it. He would abide by Elizabeth's own independent decision—he could not accept the judgment of anyone else on such a vital matter. His whole life, all he was and ever hoped to be, was in the hollow of her hand.

Then it was Elizabeth in her usual quiet voice gave him the answer which her conviction forced upon her and spoke the words which made both of their lives a sacrifice upon the altar of duty. Johns knew Elizabeth and he knew her decision was final. This girl, like his uncle Gerard, was made of stern stuff, though in manner so gentle and womanly. He had no words with which to meet the situation. A silence fell between them. Woman-like, Elizabeth took the matter in her own hands. She told him how dependent she was upon him, and said that he must not forsake her because of her decision. She begged him to be to her as he had been these seven years. She told him she would never marry, and that as long as he needed her companionship or advice she would be near to give it.

So ended the one real love of Johns Hopkins's life and so began the unusual friendship between these two which lasted as long as they lived. Neither Johns nor Elizabeth Hopkins ever married, and there is no doubt that their lives were blighted by this disappointment. They continued to see each other constantly, and the two families were always on extremely friendly terms.

In his will Johns Hopkins left Elizabeth the house in which she lived, which had come to him from his father's estate, and was located at the northeast corner of St. Paul and Franklin streets.

To the decision of this Quaker girl of long ago later generations are indebted. Denied the interests of family life, the energies of Johns Hopkins were diverted into other channels and he amassed a fortune with which he endowed the two institutions devoted to the interests of humanity. Elizabeth lived to be eighty-eight years of age, and in 1890 died in the house Johns Hopkins had given her.

After his unsuccessful courtship of his cousin, Johns himself went to Beltzoover's Hotel, on Baltimore street, to live and remained here until an attack of cholera nearly cost him his life. He then went to live in one of the two houses on Franklin and St. Paul streets left him by his father, taking his two brothers with him. Here he remained until 1843 when his mother's failing health made it advisable for her to be near a physician. He then bought a large house on Lombard Street, the second door east of Sharp street, and brought his mother and his two sisters, Hannah and Eliza, to live with him there. His mother died here in 1849 at the age of 90. This house was later used as the maternity hospital. After the death of his mother Johns Hopkins bought and occupied the fine colonial mansion at 18 W. Saratoga street, taking with him his two sisters. His sister Hannah was particularly devoted to him. She kept house for him, was untiring

MRS. SAMUEL HOPKINS, (HANNAH JANNEY), THE MOTHER OF
JOHNS HOPKINS
From a portrait now in the Johns Hopkins University

in ministering to his health and happiness, and often
sat up late listening to his account of the affairs of the
day. Eliza married a Mr. Crenshaw, but returned to
live with her brother after the death of her husband.

Though he remained a bachelor all his days, Johns
Hopkins had the greatest respect for marriage. In
reply to his nephew, Joseph Hopkins, who once asked
him why he had never married, he said that, having
failed to win the woman he loved, he felt it would be
wrong for him to marry, as he might not be true to the
ties. He felt that marriage was a sacred institution,
and although he did not specially inquire into the
morals of young men who were single, yet as a matter
of business principle he never gave a position of trust
to a man whom he knew to be lax in his morals after
marriage. He considered such conduct a breach of
contract.

CHAPTER FOUR

The Making of a Financier

THE cordial relations which for seven years had existed between Gerard Hopkins and his nephew had been interrupted. Following upon the unfortunate love affair with Elizabeth, there came other disagreements and finally a breach.

Gerard Hopkins was devoted to the work of preaching and went on many visits to Quaker meetings in various parts of the neighboring country. His nephew spoke very frankly to him on this subject telling him that if he did not stay at home and pay more attention to his business affairs the results would be disastrous.

The older man disregarded this advice, and Johns Hopkins was not one to allow things to interfere with his purposes. He felt that he had given his best efforts to his uncle, and that the firm had flourished in consequence; he did not propose now to let it suffer while he was connected with it. Also, there were certain questions upon which the older man and his young nephew did not agree. Times had become very hard, yellow fever was raging, and money was scarce. Out-of-town customers, who found it hard to pay cash, proposed that they should pay for goods by shipping whiskey in return. Johns Hopkins felt that this was legitimate, and was willing that they should do so; but his uncle felt differently and declared that he would never consent to thus "sell souls into perdition." They decided to separate and Johns Hopkins withdrew from the firm.

This break, which did not seem to affect the friendship existing between the young man and his uncle's family was, however, very significant in its consequences. Johns Hopkins was now in a position to develop his business genius unhampered, and he did so in a swift, sure, and brilliant manner. After a short partnership with a certain Benjamin Moore, which was almost immediately dissolved, he decided to go into business for himself, and, taking his three brothers, Philip, Gerard, and Mahlon, as salesmen, he formed the wholesale Provision House of "Hopkins Brothers." This house soon did a large business, especially through North Carolina and the valley of Virginia, where they had important connections. The new firm took whiskey in return for goods and sold it under the brand of "Hopkins' Best."

This action on the part of Johns Hopkins offended the Society of Friends and he was temporarily turned out of Meeting. He continued to sell whiskey, never-the-less; but he went regularly to meeting, continued to contribute and was later reinstated. In his later life, however, he felt that he had been wrong in the stand he had taken; and he told his nephew, Joseph Hopkins, that he wished he had never sold liquor, and that in so doing he had made the greatest mistake of his life.

Meanwhile Gerard Hopkins was not ungenerous, and as a token of confidence in the new firm of Hopkins'

Brothers he indorsed for it to the extent of ten thousand dollars. Another uncle, John Janney, also lent his nephew Johns an equal amount, and Hannah Hopkins and her son, Joseph, felt that they could use the money they had made on the sale of the three years' tobacco crop in no better way than by investing it in the new firm. Johns Hopkins was thus an exception to the rule that a prophet is not without honor save in his own country, for his family seemed to have unbounded confidence in his ability from the first. He thus started in business with a credit of thirty thousand dollars, which was a large sum in those days.

The facts are thus not in accord with the popular idea that the great financier started as a penniless, uneducated youth and single-handed conquered the financial world. On the contrary, he had a background of ancestry of which he might be proud, the business experience of seven years in a large wholesale house, and a capital of something more than thirty thousand dollars; for he had himself saved up a thousand dollars while in business with his uncle.

Johns Hopkins had what might be considered an instinct for business; he always seemed to see a little farther in financial matters than other men. Personal economy and extreme care in details were combined in him with great energy and endurance, and also with a vision which foresaw possibilities and made him willing to be liberal in matters of importance. His methods were bold and self-reliant, often high-handed; yet he invariably carried his point, sometimes leaving others to see the wisdom of it later. He remained connected with the firm of Hopkins Brothers for twenty-five years, and then retired, leaving the business to his brothers. During this time, though the city passed through several periods of great financial depression, this firm was looked upon as one whose methods were irreproachable and whose credit was unquestioned. Unfortunately, the death of Gerard Hopkins at the early age of twenty-five and of Philip and Mahlon each in their thirty-sixth year brought the business of Hopkins Brothers to an untimely close. Gerard was killed by a stray stone thrown by street rioters when he happened to be passing.

When Johns Hopkins had once satisfied himself that an investment was justified, he opened his coffers and gave freely. He lent money all over the city, his business developed rapidly into that of a banker, and he soon became the leading capitalist of Baltimore. Because of his insight into human nature and his accurate judgment of the characters of men, Johns Hopkins became an exceptional judge of credit. He became acquainted with the financial standing of every business house in the city of Baltimore, and made a practice of buying up, at a low figure, notes which had become overdue. He selected those which he felt from his knowledge of the firms would eventually be paid, and he seldom made a mistake. He also endorsed for many business houses in which he had confidence and which were willing to pay well for the use of his name. Though he undoubtedly added to his fortune

in this way, after the Civil War he lent his name freely
and without profit for many struggling firms in sore
need of financial backing, and so kept them from going
on the rocks. Many young men in Baltimore and
elsewhere were helped to their start in life by Johns
Hopkins.

In his early career this unassuming Quaker showed
a breadth of vision far beyond the average, and later
as a banker his attitude was such as is found to-day
only in the most progressive cities of the United States.
While his mercantile and banking business occupied
him constantly, Johns Hopkins ever bore in mind the
welfare of his native city. There were in his time few
buildings adequate for the transaction of the business
of a rapidly growing city. He purchased lots in the
business section upon which he built large warehouses,
as well as other buildings of a more ornamental character, thus substantially directing and aiding the ever-
increasing trade of the city. Though he was by nature
extremely careful and deliberate, yet when his imagination was fired, he rushed in where less courageous souls
feared to tread. His greatest adventure was the
Baltimore and Ohio railroad. Sponsoring the untried
venture of a railroad in those days was even more of a
risk than backing aviation to-day. Such was the
prejudice against this new enterprise that in the early
days of Johns Hopkins's business career an Ohio school
board refused the use of its school-house for a lecture
on the subject of railroads. They declared that there
could be no such thing as a railroad and if there were,

CONESTOGA WAGON, USED FOR FREIGHT
By courtesy of the Baltimore "Sun"

"it must be a wicked, sacrilegious and blasphemous thing, since there was no warrant for it in Holy Writ." Yet this cautious and somewhat circumscribed man, who had scarcely ever been outside of his own town, was from its very incipiency keenly interested in the new enterprise and wide awake as to its possibilities.

That Johns Hopkins should promptly recognize the promise in the proposed railway connection for Baltimore was not surprising. His great Conestoga wagons, each crammed with sufficient merchandise to fill a small warehouse, with their spanking four- and six-horse teams and jingling bells, were crossing and re-crossing the Alleghanies to the new States beyond; and far down the newly accessible Valley of Virginia his firm was a household name. On one occasion he sent a load of merchandise weighing four tons to Mount Vernon, Ohio, a distance of four hundred miles. The wagon brought back three tons and a half of Ohio tobacco.

Throwing himself heart and soul into the new enterprise, Johns Hopkins became at once a large stockholder. In 1847 he was induced to become a director of the Baltimore and Ohio road, and in 1855 he was elected chairman of the Finance Committee and became the real directing power behind the throne, with a private holding of between 15,000 and 17,000 shares of the Company's stock.

During his connection with the Baltimore and Ohio railroad he was always ready to come to its assistance, and in the panics of 1857 and 1873 he pledged his private fortune to the road endorsing for it to the large amount of about a million dollars, thus enabling it to maintain its credit.

Johns Hopkins remained the chairman of the Finance Committee until his death, and it was not until after this event, that, by a policy of extension, the road got into great financial embarrassment. In the panic of 1873 Johns Hopkins voluntarily came forward and by his individual efforts and the support of his large credit protected this road as well as the city of Baltimore from the financial disaster which struck such heavy blows to the neighboring communities of Philadelphia and New York. Such public-spirited conduct in times of stress, was not new in the life of Johns Hopkins. During the period of the Civil War, he had similarly exerted himself to promote the security of Baltimore. George W. Brown, Mayor of the city in 1861 has left the following account in his book, *Baltimore, the 19th of April 1861:* "Saturday, April the 20th, 1861, about 10 A.M., the City Council assembled immediately and appropriated $500,000 to be expended under my direction as Mayor, for the purpose of putting the city in a completed state of defense against any description of danger arising or which might arise out of the present crisis. The Banks of the City promptly held a meeting, and a few hours afterward a Committee appointed by them, consisting of three bank Presidents, Johns Hopkins, John Clark, Columbus O'Donnell, all wealthy Union men, placed the whole sum in advance at my disposal."

For many years Johns Hopkins was President of

the Merchants' Bank and Director in many others—the First National, The Mechanics, the Central, The National Union, The Citizens and Farmers, and The Farmers' and Planters.' He was also Treasurer of The Republic Life Insurance Company of Chicago, Director of The Baltimore Warehouse Company, and The Merchants' Mutual Marine Insurance Company. He was, indeed, one of the greatest financial authorities of his day. A contemporary says of him:—

"Mr. Hopkins is of an old and respectable Quaker family from the adjoining county of Anne Arundel, and came to Baltimore in 1812 and entered upon a mercantile career which by his sagicity, frugality and energy, has developed into a success unexampled in the history of the city. While amassing a fortune, collossal in its dimensions, he has kept steadily in view the prosperity and advancement of Baltimore, and has contributed greatly to the improvement of the city by fostering her commercial interests, erecting solid and substantial edifices for her increasing trade, and extending timely and judicious aid to her young and enterprising merchants and manufacturers.

"The material assistance he granted to the Baltimore and Ohio Railroad in the hours of darkness which shrouded that corporation prior to 1857, is deserving of special mention. Mr. Hopkins indorsed paper of the corporation to a large amount, and pledged his private fortune in support of the Company's interests. The present conditions of that great organization fully attest his sagacity; and to the judgment which led him to embark his capital in the fortunes of this company, is due much of the success which has attended his subsequent business career. He . . . proposes to crown a useful life by conferring upon the country in which he made it, the perpetual benefit of much the larger portion of his great fortune."

From the early days of his financial success Johns Hopkins looked upon his wealth as a trust of which he must make such use as would benefit his relatives and others than himself. With this in mind he frequently talked with others of his ideas, notably with Dr. Parker, of Philadelphia, and with Mr. George Peabody. These two men gave him encouragement in the plans which were slowly formulating themselves in his mind.

The love of learning which had been fostered in him by his mother and also by the English Master of South River School had made him unusually appreciative of education, and the fact that he himself had been obliged to leave school so early and to become largely self-educated turned his attention toward the establishment of a university. He wanted to help young men in every way he could, and this was the way which especially recommended itself and in a measure compensated for his own lack of opportunity.

There was another field in which Johns Hopkins felt that his fellow man greatly needed assistance. He had many times during his life seen the city thrown into a frenzy of grief and fear by the terrible epidemics of smallpox, cholera, and yellow fever which reappeared with appalling frequency; and he had observed the helplessness of the people and of the doctors in the face of these scourges. In this day of magnificent hospitals and trained nurses and of the discoveries in science which have enabled doctors to cope successfully with contagious diseases, it is almost impossible for the imagination to picture the misery of those early times.

Johns Hopkins had himself fallen a victim of cholera at one time and had felt the effects of it the rest of his life. Many persons were no doubt killed by the treatment rather than by the disease. In the case of both yellow fever and cholera frequent bleeding was prescribed until the patient had lost from four to five pounds of blood. Calomel was given every two hours for several days in doses of from twenty to twenty-six grains each. Dense ignorance prevailed as to the cause and the cure of contagious disease. The people resorted to the most absurd measures which they thought purified the air. Some tied tarred ropes around their necks, and others lighted bon-fires at the street corners; physicians advised the burning of gunpowder and many citizens resorted to the repeated firing of guns.

As late as 1832, during an epidemic of cholera in Baltimore, nurses could not be found and the city called upon the Sisters of Charity. There were no available hospitals and the colored people and poorer whites were taken to a camp hastily provided in the suburbs. Finding that many of the sick were literally being turned into the street, Archbishop Whitfield offered his residence on the corner of Charles and Mulberry (later the residence of the Cardinal) as a temporary hospital.

Having been a witness to such desperate conditions Johns Hopkins felt that there was a very urgent need of a modern hospital with facilities for research work, a training school for nurses, and wards to accommodate the poor of the city. To the perfecting of his plan to secure these advantages for Baltimore he devoted the latter years of his life.

CHAPTER FIVE

ANECDOTES

MOST of us are made up of contradictions, and so was Johns Hopkins. In spite of his broad outlook and his many generosities he was, in small things, over-careful and economical. He was lavish and yet penurious; he gave with one hand bountifully and held back with the other unaccountably. During the most impressionable years of his life he saw his parents practising rigid economy to enable them to recuperate from the loss of their slaves. What was more natural than that habits of petty economy should cling to him through life! He could lend a million dollars from his private fortune to help the Baltimore and Ohio Railroad out of a difficulty, open his coffers freely to avert a panic from Baltimore, and yet when it was suggested to him that his town house needed recarpeting he hesitated, because, as he explained, he hated to lose the interest on the money it would require. In later life after he had decided to endow a hospital and a university it was noticed by his family that these habits of small economies increased. In his dress Johns Hopkins was always careless; he had to be urged to buy a new suit and never wore an overcoat even on the coldest days. Yet in the furnishing of his city and country residences he had been magnificent, importing statuary, paintings, and china in

41

profusion, as well as rare shrubs, plants, and trees for
his gardens. His table was luxurious and his dinner
parties famous. Though trained from childhood to
habits of economy, and brought up in the austere
principles of the Society of Friends, Johns Hopkins
was no ascetic. He believed in enjoying the good
things of life and saw no harm in many of them which
his church, at that time, frowned upon. He liked good
wine and always had the best upon his table. His
instincts were social and he entertained many of the
interesting people who visited Baltimore. He was
especially fond of hearing descriptions of other countries from those who had visited them. He could have
traveled himself, and few people would have appreciated foreign countries with as much intelligence; yet
he never seems to have gone further away from home
than to make a visit to Cape May with his nephew,
Lewis Hopkins on occasions, when his one physical
weakness, insomnia, became unbearable. Speaking of
Johns Hopkins, a cousin of his who knew him well says:

"Cousin Johns was a clannish man. He liked to
gather his family about him and his entertainments
for them were quite as elaborate as for strangers.
Family dinners used to last for hours, course after
course, with all sorts of the finest wines. My brother
and I were Friends and not accustomed to wine at
home; taking a drink of champagne on one occasion my
brother innocently remarked, 'This is very fine cider!'
Cousin Johns looked at him rather searchingly, smiled,
and said nothing. Johns Hopkins was really a very

face — hoping to be
given a ready response
Prof. Caten before the
first of March

— the [Probably a teacher?]
to my Nephew — Marten
Hopkins — my brother am;
son. he is a robust
exemplary young man
of great personal purity
and promise — being
highly educated — and
will be well adapted
to the Critic. to Ministering
a community as that
of our neighbourhood
— Please let me hear
from this at thy earliest
convenience —

with high regard
thy friend & relative
John Hopkins

Please make such
an arrangement — as
there will be no mis
take a disappoint
ment on the part
the boys & ministry

generous man and liked to see people enjoy life and
amuse themselves. I was very fond of him. He used
to come to see his grandfather, Joseph Janney, very
often, especially after the old man had been paralyzed.
He came often, also, to see my mother, a cousin of
whom he was very fond, and I think it was on her
account that he left my father, who was only a cousin
by marriage, the treasurership of the Johns Hopkins
Hospital with a salary of several thousand dollars a
year, as long as my father lived.

"A love of children was a marked characteristic of
Cousin Johns and when a little child happened to be
at his table he always had a high chair placed next to
himself. One of his chief interests in life seemed to be
his numerous nieces and nephews. He always had
some of them staying at Clifton, enjoyed seeing them
have a good time, and was constantly helping them in
one way or another."

Johns Hopkins never hesitated, however, to set his
nieces and nephews down if he felt that they deserved
it, and in doing so he sometimes displayed his keen
sense of humor. He was in the habit of giving each of
the young people of the family a small amount of money
at Christmas. As they grew older, some of them felt
that it was too little and that their rich uncle should
give them more. These put their heads together and
decided to give "Uncle Johns" an unusually nice
present at Christmas and make him ashamed of giving
them such small ones. When the presents were handed
him, their uncle received the gifts with great apprecia-

tion, saying how very nice it was of them to think so much of their uncle, "But," said he, "I do not feel that my small gifts are any longer needed," and thereafter they received no Christmas presents from him. Those who had sent him nothing, however, received a larger gift than usual. He was not to be dictated to.

Johns Hopkins was as careful in buying a small tract of land as he would have been in financing an international loan. Indeed, extreme and searching care of details was his constant practice. The following letter to Edward Stabler of Sandy Spring, Maryland illustrates this point:

Baltimore, January 2, 1863.

My valued friend:

I thank thee kindly for the promptness with which thee has responded to my request regarding the Bready farm and have made up my mind to ask thee to make the purchase—say $50 per acre the land of course to be measured—I propose to pay one half in Cash—and if convenient to the seller to pay the remainder in 12 months with interest—I think he should make no charge for any crop that may be in the ground nor for any manure there may be in the Barn yard—possession to be given as early as possible not later than the first of March—this property is purchased for my Nephew Mahlon Hopkins—my brother Sam's son. He is a most exemplary young man of great personal purity and promise—being highly educated—and will be well adapted to enter so meritorious a community as that of your neighborhood—please let me hear from thee at thy earliest convenience —with high regards thy friend and relative Johns Hopkins.

Please make such an arrangement as there can be no mistake or disappointment, as the party thee says is unsteady.

Joseph Hopkins, a nephew of Johns Hopkins, who spent much time at Clifton and was a favorite of his uncle says of him:

"Though in many enterprises Uncle Johns was the power behind the throne, he did not seem to care for personal prominence but preferred to act quietly, through others, rather than to appear himself, and to put things through without seeming to be doing so. I was staying at Clifton, where I spent my summers when a boy, and my cousin, Ned Janney, was there too. We knew that Uncle Johns wanted Mr. John Garrett to be president of the Baltimore and Ohio Railroad. There was a great deal of opposition to this among the directors of the road; but I knew that Uncle Johns had determined to put it through and was anxious to see how he would do it. He told Ned and me he was going to have a dinner for the directors of the road and they wanted us to get some frogs for them. We worked hard all one morning and got fifty frogs from the pond at Clifton. The old gentleman was so pleased that he invited us to the dinner. We were very much set up, as we knew an important move would be made and we had a great deal of curiosity to see how Uncle Johns would get his way with the opposing directors.

"Champagne and other wines flowed freely during the dinner and Jim kept filling our glasses. I never knew exactly what happened, but just about the time that things seemed to be getting interesting Ned and I were quietly taken away from the table.

"I was always sorry that we were obliged to leave

and have often wondered since how Uncle Johns
managed to put this thing through.

"The next day there was no one at the dinner table
but the family. I never took a dinner at Clifton,
however, when there was not Champagne, whether
company was there or not. Jim started to fill my glass
and I put my hand over it. 'Take thy hand off thy
glass, Joe,' said Uncle Johns. 'Let the wine stand if
thee does not want it, but don't publish thy temperance
resolves.' Uncle Johns hated any show of superiority
and never made any himself; on the contrary, he was
apt to relate anecdotes which were not flattering to his
vanity and enjoyed the humor of them even though it
was at his own expense. On one occasion when an
out-of-town cousin was visiting Clifton, the butler was
about to fill his glass with wine when the young man
remarked, 'No, thank you, I do not drink.' Uncle
Johns said, 'Jim, fill his glass. Now, if thee doesn't
care to drink it thee doesn't have to do so.' Any
signs of setting oneself up above others annoyed him.
He never denied his own frailties and although he was
a man of great dignity, when he was in the humor
he could make himself extremely entertaining and
agreeable."

Perhaps Johns Hopkins would have liked to have
a little more fun sometimes than was consistent with
the custom of Friends in those days. At one time he
wanted to put a billiard-table in his town-house on
Saratoga Street. He invited a Mr. Tabb to see him
one evening and asked him what he thought of a

JOSEPH S. HOPKINS, A FAVORITE NEPHEW OF JOHNS HOPKINS

certain room in the house for that purpose. To his surprise, Mr. Tabb said, "Johns, I don't think your mother would have liked it." Needless to say, the billiard-table was never put in. He was devoted to his mother and always had the greatest respect for her opinion. When her health began to fail, he bought the large house on Lombard Street. Many of the old substantial families of Baltimore lived in this neighborhood at that time. Later, after the death of his mother, Johns Hopkins bought the large colonial house, 18 West Saratoga Street, just opposite the Hotel Rennert (since built) which is now occupied by the Royal Arcanum. Here he lived until his death. His sisters all married excepting Hannah, who kept house for him as long as she lived. His sister, Eliza, Mrs. Crenshaw, also came and lived with him after the death of her husband.

In business Johns Hopkins was independent and even high-handed. Again quoting Joseph Hopkins:

"Uncle Johns' brother, Uncle Samuel, did not go into the firm of Hopkins Brothers when that firm was inaugurated, but associated himself with a man named Matthews in the lumber business in Woodberry. This business got into bad shape and Matthews and Hopkins were about to dissolve. Uncle Johns overhauled the business, settled it up, and then, without consulting his brother, published in the paper that Samuel Hopkins was dissolving partnership with Matthews, and that he had become a member of the firm of Hopkins Brothers. This meant that Uncle Johns had taken his brother into his firm and had saved him financially. He had done it without consulting Uncle Samuel, who was not at all pleased at the high-handed proceeding; however, instead of being ruined he later retired worth a hundred thousand dollars, a fortune in those days."

As a further illustration of Johns Hopkins' method of getting his own way Mr. Charles G. Baldwin relates the following incident:

"My mind goes back to a hot day in the 50's. . . . . The richest man in Baltimore passed down Liberty Street on a summer day, turned into Baltimore Street, down Hanover Street to the corner of German Street and walked into the firm of Woodward, Jones and Company, Dry Goods Commission Merchants. Back in the counting room was a young man in his shirt sleeves and a number of clerks. Everybody knew Mr. Hopkins, and everybody stopped what he was doing to look at him, and listened to every word. It was the first time that this man, who was President of the Merchants' Bank, Director of the B & O Railroad, Chairman of its Finance Committee, leading Abolitionist, hated and discounted by the slave owners, who constituted the bulk of the leading men of the city, had ever entered the office of Woodward, Jones and Company.

"The young man in shirt sleeves was William Henry Baldwin, Jr. He jumped up somewhat embarrassed. Their families had been neighbors in Anne Arundel County. . . . . The Prince of Wales was in Baltimore. Had *he* come into the Counting House Baldwin would not have been more surprised.

The Hopkins Mansion at 18 West Saratoga Street; The House in Which Johns Hopkins Died in 1873

"'Henry, can thee go out with me to the Savage Factory to attend an auction sale? I want thee to bid on it.'

"'Certainly, Mr. Hopkins. Anything I can do for you I am glad to do.'

"'Put on thy coat and come along.'

"On the train the conductor was most obsequious. He did not even ask Mr. Baldwin for his fare. Everybody either loved or hated Johns Hopkins, and those who hated him feared to show their hatred because they well knew his power. They saved it up until after he was dead.

"'Going, going, gone! William Henry Baldwin for $40,000, Savage Factory. Mr. Baldwin, I congratulate you upon your purchase!' said the auctioneer.

"'Henry,' said Mr. Hopkins, 'thee has a cheap property.'

"Mr. Baldwin had made the bid at the request of Mr. Hopkins, and thought the bid was made for Mr. Hopkins. His jaw dropped. The hot sun made him take off his coat. His shoulders are said to have drooped to such an extent that his suspenders rolled down upon his sides.

"'Why, Mr. Hopkins, I have not $10,000 in the world! How can I buy this factory? You asked me to put in these bids. *You* are the mortgagee. *You* are the owner of the Savage Factory.'

"'No, Henry, thee bid for it, and the factory is thine; but I will stand by thee in this matter for I know thee is the proper person to own this factory.'

"Poor Henry! As much as he admired Johns Hopkins, was not able to overcome the surprise and fears and anxieties which seemed to overwhelm him. After a good night's rest, however, he determined to make the most of the situation and to assume the property. He gave it all the energy and ability at his command, and in a few years had built up a successful factory in place of one which had been deserted.

"Johns Hopkins made him a director of the Merchants' Bank and was always ready with advice and assistance.

"This hot day's work was the cornerstone of the fortune of William Henry Baldwin, Jr.

"There is still another incident I should like to record: My father, Summerfield Baldwin, was a young merchant in Baltimore and went into partnership with the late Edward T. Norris. His contribution toward the capital of the firm was $600 in savings, $1100, borrowed from his brother, Columbus C. Baldwin, and a good reputation in the business community. Mr. Norris contributed about the same, and when the paper was presented at the Merchants' Bank for discount, with Johns Hopkins at the head of the board, who passed it around the table, it did not go very far before one of the members turned it down. According to the custom of the bank this meant that the loan would not be granted. When the notes came back to Mr. Hopkins, he carefully looked them over, and finding that the note of Baldwin and Norris had been turned down for discount, he wrote his name upon the back of it and passed it around again. Needless to say, when it came back this time it had not been turned down, and from that day to this millions of dollars of the firm have been passed by this board without any question, much to the financial benefit of myself and family."

In 1857 a panic due to yellow fever caused great uneasiness in the business world. Johns Hopkins's indebtedness was almost entirely to the Union Bank of Baltimore and they called upon him to pay it off. He went to a meeting of the directors of the bank and put before them very plainly what would happen if they called on him to pay, saying, "Gentlemen, if you insist upon my paying, you will break your bank." With this he abruptly put on his hat and left. Finding that what he said was perfectly true, the president granted him an extension. When the yellow fever abated and the panic was over Johns Hopkins paid off all his indebtedness to the Union Bank.

Later on when the president got into some financial embarrassment Johns Hopkins in gratitude for his help during such an anxious period sent him a check for ten thousand dollars.

The strain of this time, however, had been very hard on Mr. Hopkins and he went to bed exhausted after working night and day. His health had never been the same since an attack of cholera, contracted in 1832, had resulted in a very severe illness. He did not sleep for nearly two weeks at that time, and his doctor said that if this continued he would die. Although this contingency was averted, insomnia became one of the things that he had to fight against the rest of his life.

Many a friendly act is remembered of Johns Hopkins toward young men, but he hid his kind heart under a blunt and curt way of dealing that was often misunderstood. When a well-known Baltimorean of the last generation was just starting in business he wanted to borrow money of his older friend, Mr. Hopkins, who had the reputation of always being ready to help a deserving young man. With this in mind, the youth decided to approach Mr. Hopkins some morning on his way to the office. Noticing the time when his older friend usually left the house, he one day dressed himself up rather elegantly and seeing the tall man with his swinging gait approaching, went up to him and in a pleasant voice said, "Good morning, Mr. Hopkins, how are you to-day?"

"Oh, very well, thank thee, Dick, what does thee want?" was the unexpected reply.

Surprised and a little nettled at being so quickly discovered in his plans, the young man replied a little hesitatingly, "Why, I was thinking of asking you for a loan."

Johns Hopkins cast a searching look at the immaculate clothes and said, "Go home, Dick, and take off those fine clothes. Then come to my office and I will talk to thee about it."

The crest-fallen youth did go home, but pride prevented him from again going to see the man who had set him down. In a little while, however, there came a message that Mr. Hopkins would like to see him at the office. This time he put on the oldest clothes he possessed, and, pulling a shabby hat over his eyes, proceeded to the well-known office. He was received cordially and Mr. Hopkins, as was his custom, went directly to the point.

"Now tell me, Dick, what can I do for thee?" said he.

Feeling that the occasion was propitious, the young man mentioned a sum which he though might make Johns Hopkins hesitate. Not so. Reaching for his check book, the older man drew up a check for the desired amount without hesitation, and handing it to his young friend said, "I don't want any interest on this, Dick. Pay me when thee gets ready."

Joseph Hopkins when a youth, meeting his Uncle Johns on the street one day, became conscious that the older man was not pleased with his appearance. "Joe" said Johns Hopkins, "I see thee has on a fine new hat; how much did thee pay for it?"

"Three dollars," replied the nephew, well knowing that he was in for a lecture; for three dollars in that day was very much more to pay for a hat than at the present time.

"Well, Joe, I do not feel that any young man has a right when starting in life to spend so much money on his personal adornment." Though Johns Hopkins often criticized or corrected his nephews, he did it in a spirit of kindly interest which they appreciated later if not always at the time.

A gentleman who was at one time associated with a

Baltimore bank tells of Johns Hopkins being present one morning when a young man came into the bank who wished to borrow money. He presented his note and credentials, but the bank, not feeling that his credit was sufficiently good, turned him down. Disappointed, the young man was about to leave when Mr. Hopkins calling to him, said, "Let me see thy note!" Taking it he wrote his own name across it. "There," said he, "perhaps that will make it more satisfactory."

The gentleman who witnessed this incident was so impressed that he followed Mr. Hopkins out of the bank and joining him said, "That was a very kind thing you just did, Mr. Hopkins."

"Nothing of the sort," replied the latter in his blunt way, "Just a good piece of business, that's all."

Mr. George Cator of Baltimore relates that a certain man at one time well known in the business world of the city wanted to save his firm by borrowing one hundred thousand dollars of the bank, which at that time charged four per cent. He had not the collateral, however, on which to borrow this money. His unfortunate predicament reached the ears of his friend, Johns Hopkins, who saved him in a most generous way by lending him Baltimore and Ohio stock amounting to one hundred thousand dollars. This stock paid six per cent and the difference between this and the bank's charges gave Johns Hopkins's friend an extra two thousand dollars a year.

Such incidents as these were typical. Upon discount

day in the different banks with which Johns Hopkins
was connected as director, he often added his signature
to the paper of young men whose future success was
not apparent to the other directors and who, largely
through the credit thus extended to them, became
prosperous business men.

A story which illustrates very well the conflicting
instincts of generosity and parsimony which often made
Johns Hopkins seem strangely contradictory has been
related by his sister-in-law, the wife of his brother,
Joseph. Walking into his office one day, she explained
to Johns Hopkins the needs of a certain home for aged
colored women and asked him for a contribution. He
hesitated a little and said he was very busy but, seeing
that she persisted, finally said that he had very little
money in the safe. She was not to be so easily set
aside in her purpose and seeing this, he said,

"Well, Elizabeth, how much does thee think I ought
to give?"

"We need a thousand dollars, Johns," was the
quick reply.

"Then I shall have to give it to thee some other time,
I never keep so much money on hand."

"Thy note will be all that is necessary, Johns,"
she ventured, feeling that there was no time like the
present. He finally assented to this, made out his
note for one thousand dollars, and handed it to her.
Feeling that he had been generous, she thanked him
accordingly and was leaving the office when he called
her back.

"Elizabeth, what is thee going to do with that note?"

"Why, take it to bank, Johns, and have it discounted."

"How much will that cost thee?"

"Six per cent, that is sixty dollars, and I shall have nine hundred and forty dollars left."

"Well, Elizabeth, I guess that I can do that for thee as well as the bank," he replied. He proceeded to do so, discounted his own note, and saved the sixty dollars.

Johns Hopkins was devoted to country life. His greatest delight and recreation was his country place on the Harford Road, Clifton. He bought it at an auction sale from a prominent merchant who had failed, and gradually purchased land adjacent until he had an estate of over five hundred acres. The old house was remodeled and enlarged in Italian villa style, as it is at present. He put in very handsome imported Italian mantel-pieces, many fine statues and vases and had the walls of the main halls and rooms frescoed by a foreign artist of prominence who happened to be in this country. Fowler, the old Scottish gardener, had been educated in horticulture on the estate of the Duke of Buccleuch and was very successful in beautifying Clifton. It became the show place of Baltimore, and every stranger who went sight-seeing was taken there.

When the Prince of Wales, afterward King Edward the VII, visited Baltimore, he spent part of an afternoon at Clifton. Persons who wished to visit Clifton secured tickets of admission at Mr. Hopkins's office at the bank. When anyone of prominence or a personal friend, came, after being shown around the grounds, he was asked to the house where some of the rare fruits were offered him. It was the dearest wish of Johns Hopkins's heart that the University which bears his name should be located at Clifton, and he took an especial interest in the planting and the developing of the grounds with this in mind.

CHAPTER SIX

JOHNS HOPKINS AT HOME

CLIFTON had never looked more lovely. The great magnolia grandifloras were in full bloom, their glossy leaves towering above the old gardener's cottage and the huge white blossoms filling the air with exotic perfume. In the distance glimmered the blue waters of the Patapsco, and in the foreground the swans glided with arched necks upon the lake.

Johns Hopkins loved it; the pure beauty of the scene satisfied a certain craving in the depths of his nature, a craving that had been bred and nurtured in the sunny fields of Anne Arundel in the old fox-hunting days of his boyhood, and that still survived in spite of the heavy responsibilities and the ceaseless drive of a successful business career. He turned and looked at the old house, satisfying in its dignified simplicity, its ample proportions, and its beautiful setting. This was his child; he had created it and watched the planting of each tree and shrub. He and Fowler, the old Scottish gardener, had had many a consultation as to the placing of each group of flowering things. Fowler was a man of intelligence and ability. Indeed, he had been the means of bringing the truest pleasure and the most genuine recreation into the life of this overworked man of affairs. Here at Clifton Johns Hopkins could usually sleep, though frequently even here he read far

CLIFTON—THE COUNTRY HOME OF JOHNS HOPKINS—NOW A CITY PARK

into the night or paced the long porches before "the tight-closed lips" and "iron eyes" of sleep relaxed and his brain stopped its incessant working.

Yes, Fowler deserved great credit, he was entitled to a certain amount of his employer's confidence and friendship. Thinking along these lines the tall man swung quickly around and with the strong stride of one full of vigor and purposeful confidence made his way across the great stretch of lawn, down the avenue of stately trees to the little brick house under the magnolias. A decided rap on the door immediately brought an energetic, pleasant-faced old Scotchman to answer it.

"Fowler," said the big man, waving his stick toward the hills at the far end of the grounds, "come and take a walk with me, I have something to talk over with thee."

Passing the old grapery, where bunches of Black Hamburgs hung in luscious clusters, and passing the nectarine trees and the fig bushes, the owner cast an approving look.

"They're doing well this year, Fowler; in fact, the whole place is a great satisfaction to me, and few could have done as well with it as thee has."

The old gardener's face lighted up. Mr. Hopkins did not often express appreciation, but somehow a word now and then made all those who worked for him his willing servants. Up at the big house Aunt Chloe well knew that the trouble she took in preparing some unusually tasty meal was never overlooked or wasted.

Jim, the butler, and Charles understood very well that, though often silent, Mr. "Johnsie" never failed to give some token of approval when they had done their best.

Together the two men made their way to the brow of the hill and turned to look back over the panorama that stretched before them. Johns Hopkins spoke of far-reaching plans that lay back in his mind, while the old gardener swelled with pride. So this was to be not just a beautiful country home; his efforts were leading on to something bigger and greater; and while he listened he felt that he was a part of all these things to be, and as the wonder of it dawned upon him, his blood flowed faster and his eyes shone brighter.

"This estate, Fowler, is to be the site of a great university, a place where the young men of coming generations will have the opportunity which I have always longed for. Young men will study great things here under these trees that thee and I have planted, and yonder, over nearer to the Patapsco, will be a great hospital. On the brow of this hill where we are standing will be the main buildings of the university, with a wide avenue connecting the university with the hospital. I have thought it all out, Fowler. All my family shall be taken care of according to their needs, but after that is done all I own shall go to these two children of mine, a university and a hospital. Like the man in the parable, I have had many talents given to me and I feel that they are in trust; I shall not bury them but give them to the lads who long for a wide education and who will do great things some day with

The Lodge and Gateway to Clifton.   Destroyed When Clifton Became a Public Park

the knowledge they receive here in this university. Thee knows, Fowler, for thee has seen me surrounded for years by my nieces and nephews, that I have a great fondness for young people and a great sympathy especially with young men who are ambitious to make their mark in the world. Well, they shall have a chance right here under the shadow of these old trees."

Slowly they walked home again, Johns Hopkins still talking and confiding his treasured plans to the willing ears of his faithful friend and helper.

When they reached the little cottage, they paused to look at the rare plants and shrubs so carefully nursed and cherished—a bond of sympathy between the two these many years.

Two boys came running across the lawn claiming their "Uncle Johns" for the evening meal and escorting him back to the big house. Here they were joined by Hannah and Eliza, sisters of Johns, who made a pretty picture standing at the top of the long veranda steps their gray silk gowns, made simply in Quaker fashion with white tulle kerchiefs crossed in front and caps of the same material tied under the chin with white ribbons. In a quiet and affectionate manner they greeted their brother and led him off to the great dining-room where they were soon joined by several pretty nieces, one of whom had to sit on either side of her uncle, while Hannah Hopkins presided at the other end of the table. As usual, the meal did justice to Aunt Chloe's ability and kept Jim and Charles busy serving, their black faces occasionally breaking into smiles as one of the boys told a joke or Uncle Johns related an amusing story. After dinner the party wandered out on to the grass and broke up into little groups, until darkness drove them in and finally to bed.

Left alone, Johns Hopkins walked into the room he loved the best, his library, closely followed by Zeno, his faithful dog. He selected a book of travel and sank into an easy chair reading far into the night of the lands he longed to visit. Why was it that his life was so circumscribed, he wondered. He ought to have travelled, he felt; but somehow there were always so many business matters requiring his attention, and he could not bear to go away leaving loose ends. More than once he had been on the point of taking a trip of some extent but it had always ended in getting his nephew, Lewis Hopkins, to go down to Cape May with him for a couple of weeks. It was foolish to have put it off—and now, well, he felt that he would never go. He sighed deeply and Zeno looked up with a melancholy and understanding eye.

"I'll never do it now, old fellow—we're getting old, thee and I, Zeno—and I need all the money I have and all I can save for my two children, the great school and the great hospital. Too late—too late. Well, all my energies have been for local matters and perhaps it is right that it is so."

He closed his book and sinking lower in his chair gazed with his mental vision far back into the years. One thing he was thankful for, his mother had been taken care of in every way to the very best of his

Margaret Hopkins, (Mrs. Miles White), Fourth Sister of
Johns Hopkins

ability—those long years of her self-sacrifice and love
had been repaid so far as material things and his love
and consideration could ever repay them. And he
tried to do the right thing by his family to whom he was
deeply attached. He knew they sometimes felt he
might be softer, more spontaneously generous—but
wasn't it always so with a man of wealth? Unfortunately (he thought) he must always say what
he felt in direct forcible language: he couldn't smooth
things over, rub people down in the right way, or be
tactful—no, it just wasn't his way. He had been often
aware of stirrings in his nature that would have made
him different under different circumstances. He loved
children, felt that he understood them, and he loved
femininity. Perhaps he should have married—he was
a man whom women took to, and he had much to offer.
At times he had been almost on the point of asking
someone to be his wife, but he couldn't quite reconcile
himself to the fetters. It was better so—marriage was
a sacred thing; and he might have degraded it, as so
many others did. It would have been different if he
could have married Elizabeth; she could have made
him all a married man should be—but fate had not so
willed it. Thinking of what might have been, he
sighed again, glanced at the clock, and seeing that it
was past midnight, rang a bell. Jim, the faithful
darkey, soon appeared with slippers, and dressing
gown.

"I knowed you'd want these, Mr. Johnsie. Now I'll
jest git yer ready fo' bed, Suh, so as yer kin tumble

right in when yer gits sleepy, Suh, and I'll walk up and down de poach wid yer."

Out they went, and up and down the long veranda, up and down, up and down,—the white man sleepless, his brain working, working, and refusing to let go; the black man half dead with sleep, but unwilling to desert until, far into the night, he saw his master, at last physically tired, stretch out in bed and close his eyes.

CHAPTER SEVEN

LAST DAYS

THE year 1873, an eventful one for the citizens of Baltimore, started out with such intensely cold weather as had seldom been experienced in the history of the city. The thermometer fell to between ten and twenty degrees below zero. This was followed by one of the most serious panics that has ever embarrassed the financial interests of Baltimore. Later, a devastating fire consumed portions of the city and narrowly escaped destroying the residence of Johns Hopkins on Saratoga Street.

A man of seventy-eight now, Johns Hopkins through all his life had been burdened by heavy responsibilities; he had put his shoulder to the wheel in childhood and it had been there ever since. In early boyhood, when his father, by freeing all his slaves, had sacrificed the birthright of his children upon the altar of Humanity and Johns had taken upon himself his share of the work of the Plantation, he had entered upon the path which for evermore his feet must tread. As a youth in his uncle's office he felt that he must make good financially and help to lift the unaccustomed burden of poverty from his family. The War of 1812 found him in charge of a large business and left with a family of young cousins to help and protect in the absence of their parents.

The death of his father in 1814 and the untimely death of his four brothers, Gerard, Mahlon, Philip, and Joseph threw the responsibility of a large family of sisters upon him as well as the care of his mother and the guardianship of his four nephews, the children of his brother Joseph. He willingly met all these calls upon his responsibility and never seemed too burdened or too occupied with other things to devote himself to his family.

Several times during the life of Johns Hopkins a terrible scourge of yellow fever had raged in and around Baltimore, seriously interfering with the business of the city and causing great financial distress. Cholera had left its mark upon his own health, and the effects of it remained with him as a disability the rest of his life. The latter years had brought with them the peculiar horrors of the Civil War during which the neutrality of Baltimore had sometimes had to be maintained by force of arms. The Baltimore and Ohio Railroad, carrying troops on a neutral basis at a tremendous cost of anxiety to its directors threw a great burden upon Johns Hopkins, at that time chairman of its finance committee. Headed by Johns Hopkins the banks of Baltimore prepared for any distress to the city that might arise as a result of the troubled times during the war by lending to the city of Baltimore one million dollars for defence.

His Quaker instincts for peace made Johns Hopkins unusually sensitive to the useless devastation of war. He stood by the Union, was a strong Abilitionist, and his outspoken principles made him many enemies at a time when feeling ran high and every man was seeing red. He was too powerful a man to be attacked during his lifetime; but later, when death had made him defenseless, the tongues of those who would belittle him were loosed. His age, as well as his Quaker faith, prevented him from entering the War, but he did his bit to counteract its destructive effects by helping many men to regain a footing in the financial world after the fighting had ended, and by endorsing freely for young men whom he thought deserving.

In this last year of his life he early realized the serious nature of the panic, and though now an old man he once more took upon his shoulders the interests of the city. He pledged his private fortune to the merchants of Baltimore in the crisis, at the same time warning them not to sell to northern firms, and he thus saved them from disaster. He had so often put his strong mind and body to the task and had found them equal to it; but as the winter drew on he felt tired and burdened by unrelenting responsibility. A friend meeting him on the street the latter part of November inquired about his health and was surprised to hear him say,

"My end is drawing near; I am an old man and I shall not be here long. Eliza and I are very lonely in the old house, especially since Hannah has passed away. My nieces and nephews are all married and cannot be around me as before. I am lonely, and it is time for me to pass on."

Shortly after this he contracted a heavy cold and

for several days was obliged to stay in bed. He was very restless and found it impossible to get his mind off of the matters which he felt needed his presence at the office. Against the advice of his physician, Dr. W. C. VanBibber, he insisted upon getting up and going down town. As usual, he refused to wear an overcoat, or overshoes, though the weather was stormy, and the following day he became seriously ill and soon developed pneumonia.

On Christmas Eve the old man lay propped up in a four-post bed in his colonial mansion while a sweet-faced woman in Quaker costume, his sister Eliza, tripped in and out of the sick room, and Jim, the faithful servant, sat in a corner and dozed now and then for he was weary with long watching. Zeno, the dog, lay stretched on the floor at the foot of the bed. For years a constant companion, he seemed to feel that serious business was afoot and refused to be banished.

Johns Hopkins's mind was perfectly clear and his courage was unfaltering. He asked Dr. Alan Smith, who had been sent for in consultation, to tell him his true condition; and hearing that it was very serious, sent for his counsel, Mr. Charles J. M. Gwinn, and gave instructions which were to be carried out in case of his death, an event to which he seemed to be perfectly resigned.

He was aware of the presences around him and of the quiet of the room, inviting sleep. He felt weary and his mind gladly would have relaxed but as usual was insistently active. Again and again Johns Hopkins went over the events of the past years. He felt that his "house was in order," and he was ready to go. He had given careful thought and much labor to the making of his long and painstaking will. He had done for all according to their needs, taking thought of each. He had provided for his faithful servants according to their years of service, and had taken special care for the colored people, that race which in his early years on the farm, through life, and now in his last hours, had served him faithfully. In his bounties they had not been forgotten and his will carefully specified plans for an orphanage for the destitute children of this people. He had remembered the needs of such deserving institutions as The Maryland Institute, The Manual Labor School, The Home of the Friendless, and the Baltimore Orphan Asylum. It is to be noted that his beneficiaries were all institutions devoted to the care or to the education of young people. To his planning for the University and the Hospital he had given much of the latter years of his life. With careful weighing of their qualities he had appointed trustees to carry out his wishes—a group of men chosen for their intelligence, integrity, and business ability. He felt that they would be able and true to the great trust he had reposed in them, and he had written a carefully thought-out letter of instructions for their guidance.

All was in order, he felt, and he was ready for the great adventure, the only journey he had ever taken in his life. Calling his nephew, Joseph, to his bedside shortly before his death, he said: "Joe, it is very hard to break up an old habit. I've been living for seventy-eight years now, and I find it hard to make a change in my ways."

On the night of December 23, a change took place and an expression of rest and peace came over the strong features. The busy brain had at last relaxed and early on the morning of December 24 the tired body, welcoming rest, sank deeper into the pillows and fell quietly to sleep.

So passed the man who in life had denied himself much, and who, putting the needs of humanity before personal gratification, had made possible those great enterprises which, reaching down the ages, spread their benevolent effects upon his fellow men.

By the influence of the two institutions which Johns Hopkins created the character of the city has been largely influenced and Baltimore has become a center for intellectual achievement and for research work in surgery and medicine as well as in sciences and the liberal arts.

In Greenmount Cemetery a simple slab marks the grave of this benefactor, whose body lies buried in the heart of the city he loved.

JOHNS HOPKINS IN LATER LIFE

CHAPTER EIGHT

FULFILMENT

WHEN the great mechanical age began in the past century and its large industrial enterprises needed to be financed, it was to the Quakers and Dissenters, whose religion insisted upon frugality and simple ways of life, that men turned for liquid funds.

The accumulated wealth of Johns Hopkins had already been of material assistance to the City of Baltimore and the State of Maryland during Civil War days and had helped to finance a new enterprise, the Baltimore and Ohio Railroad; and now the millions he bequeathed in his will, money which had been earned through a brilliant business career and accumulated by a life of frugality, brought into being the University and the Hospital which bear his name.

It has been estimated by one whose authority on financial matters is not questioned (Dr. Jacob Hollander, of the Johns Hopkins University) that the eight million dollars left by Johns Hopkins would correspond today in purchasing power and influence to approximately one hundred million.

Johns Hopkins could not see the fulfilment of his dreams, but with rare foresight and wisdom he made his plans, chose his trustees, and wrote out detailed instructions. To his family and to various Baltimore

71

charities he left one million dollars of his estate, and
the rest he divided between the University and the
Hospital. To the University he left his estate at
Clifton and the greater part of his stock in the Baltimore and Ohio Railroad, amounting to nearly four
million dollars. To the Hospital he left a large amount
of real estate including many valuable warehouses. No
less than sixty-two of these warehouses were destroyed
in the great fire of 1904.

He chose a site for the Hospital on a direct line with
Clifton, which he had already designated as the site
of the University, and lying on the same high ridge of
land. This tract consisted of about five acres and was
the site of the old Baltimore hospital for the insane,
on Broadway, where pioneer use had been made of
vaccination, and where the wounded in the Battle of
Baltimore had been received. It was called Lauden-
slager's Hill.

In 1867 he formed two corporations, one for the
University and one for the Hospital, and three years
later he chose his trustees from among the ablest
business men of the city. For their guidance he wrote
a detailed letter of instructions, which may be found
at the end of this volume. He imposed upon them
no hampering conditions, but gave them great freedom,
insisting only on a few points which, though looked upon
then as innovations, have since proved to be judicious.
None of the principal of the endowments was to be
spent, and such buildings as were to be erected must
be financed out of the interest only. There was to be

GILMAN HALL, THE JOHNS HOPKINS UNIVERSITY

the fullest coöperation between the University and the Hospital. Nine of the twelve directors were to sit on the boards of both institutions. The hospital was to constitute a part of the medical school which was to be established by the University and which should thus link the two institutions. A training school for nurses was to be made a part of the Hospital, and a place was to be established in the country where patients who were able to do so might go to recuperate, thus leaving more room for the most serious cases. This latter provision, however, has not yet been carried out, though Clifton would seem a highly appropriate place.

The ideas of Johns Hopkins have proved eminently practical, and many of them have been adopted by institutions since founded. It has been said that, like Minerva, the institutions founded by Johns Hopkins "sprang full armed, if not full grown, from the head of their founder." The University was inaugurated February 22, 1876 by an address delivered in the Academy of Music by Thomas Huxley, the great English scientist, and instruction began in October of the same year with eighty-nine students. Mr. Daniel C. Gilman had been appointed as its first President, a man of broad interests and great tact. He was a graduate of Yale, who had won attention by an able though brief administration as president of the University of California. The opening of the Hospital was delayed for some years in order that the income, which alone could be used for buildings, might accumulate until it was possible to erect structures that embodied the latest and best designs. That was accomplished in 1889 when the formal opening of the Johns Hopkins Hospital took place.

The opening of the school of Medicine, which Johns Hopkins had directed should be established was still longer delayed. It was brought about in 1892 by a generous gift of more than $300,000 by Miss Mary Garrett.

It is not buildings or organizations which make an institution of the first order but the character of the men associated with it and of those graduated by it and sent out into the world. To Mr. Gilman is due the credit of seeing at the outset that the Johns Hopkins University could more quickly establish itself as an institution of unusually high standing by calling to its staff great men rather than by spending money on buildings, and as a university rather than as a college. His slogan was "Men, not buildings," and he wished research to form an essential part of the work of "The Hopkins."

With these ideas in mind, Mr. Gilman chose carefully those men who were to shape the policy and establish the standards of this ambitious young seat of learning. On that first staff were Basil L. Gildersleeve, the eminent Greek scholar; Ira Remsen, the chemist to whom the world is indebted for the discovery of saccharine, and who is widely known for his work on the structure of the molecule; Henry A. Rowland, the great physicist, inventor of the spectrum gratings; H. Newell Martin, the biologist; J. J. Sylvester, that brilliant mathematical giant of the Vic-

torian era, formerly professor of Mathematics at
Cambridge University, a pupil of Huxley and an expo-
nent of the great English school of biology; and
Charles D. Morris, Professor of Latin, late Fellow in
Oriel, Oxford. To this staff were soon added Richard
T. Ely and Herbert B. Adams, who presided over
political and historical studies; A. Marshall Elliott in
Romance languages; Simon Newcomb the astronomer,
and other men who made names for themselves in the
world. It is interesting to note that Woodrow Wilson,
one of the early graduates of the Johns Hopkins University, frequently returned to deliver lectures.

The Johns Hopkins became the first American
university to give the degree of Doctor of Philosophy
for accomplishment in research work. It established
an arrangement of studies which allowed wide liberty
of choice and it required two years of work, instead of
one as in most institutions, for the degree of Master
of Arts.

Its high standard brought to its doors as students
such men as Walter Hines Page, Woodrow Wilson,
William James, Albert Shaw, Josiah Royce, John H.
Finley, William Keith Brooks, Thomas Craig, Harmon
N. Morse, Richard T. Ely and Herbert B. Adams.

Strangers visiting Baltimore in the early days of the
University were amazed to find an institution of such
high reputation established in a few inconspicuous
houses on Howard Street, and Baltimoreans themselves
were bitter against the policy which had apparently
ignored the wishes of the founder and opened the

University in the heart of the city instead of at Clifton, as Johns Hopkins had planned. In the First Annual Report of the Johns Hopkins University it is stated that:

"They (the Trustees) also decided to postpone the construction of buildings at Clifton (the prospective site of the University) and to provide the requisite classrooms . . . . in the heart of the city. . . . . The Trustees have not forgotten the importance of developing the Clifton site with reference to the purposes to which it will be devoted."

Dr. A. K. Bond says in his pamphlet, "When the Hopkins Came to Baltimore," "That the Trustees did not carry out in all its details the plan of its Founder is not under criticism anywhere in this book. They were wise and able men, and I believe built better than Mr. Hopkins could have done, informing themselves as to the greater educational needs of the day. I confess, however, being somewhat of a dreamer myself, that I regret the failure of his great University Boulevard, as he saw it in his Dream."

In the early days, Clifton was used as the athletic field of the University, and a familiar sight was a four-horse Hopkins bus filled with football players going out to Clifton for practice.

It was the judgment of Mr. Gilman and a majority of the Trustees, in opposition to a strong minority, however, and to the feeling of the community in general, that conditions prevailing at the time of the opening of the University fully justified them in aban-

doning Clifton as its first site. It must be said for Mr.
Gilman that he conducted a great enterprise through
almost unequalled difficulties, and that the only
instance in which his policy was openly attacked was
the one case in which the plans and wishes of Johns
Hopkins were not adhered to.

It was pointed out that Clifton at that time, which
was in the days of horse-cars, was at an inconvenient
distance from libraries and boarding-houses and too far
out of the city to make it a desirable location, and that,
the Founder having stipulated that no building should
be done that could not be paid for out of the interest of
the endowment, it was not possible to erect sufficient
dormitories and other buildings adequate for the beginning of the University.

In 1901 the stock of the Baltimore and Ohio Railroad, owing to a policy of expansion adopted after the
death of Johns Hopkins, had fallen very low, and a
critical position for the University became evident.
The University had so outgrown the small buildings in
the city that in order to go forward it was necessary
to put up larger ones on a site which would be permanent. For this there were not sufficient funds. Mr.
Gilman, who had been President for twenty-five years,
had sent in his resignation and in many ways a turning
point had been reached. Through the munificence of
a small group of public spirited citizens, including
Mr. William Wyman, and Mr. Keyser a tract of land
in the northern section of the city was now offered to
the University as a permanent site, provided the

citizens of Baltimore would raise one million dollars with which to erect suitable buildings.

This colossal undertaking, as it seemed at that time, was successfully accomplished with the generous aid of Mr. R. Brent Keyser, Mr. Francis M. Jencks, and other citizens of Baltimore. At the same time the city offered to purchase Clifton as a public park for the generous sum of one million dollars. Clifton was sold to the city and the Johns Hopkins University moved out to its present location at "Homewood," a locality taking its name from a beautiful old Colonial mansion built there by Charles Carroll in the early days of Baltimore and still standing. This house has furnished the keynote for the architecture of the other University buildings. A surrounding park is called Wyman Park in honor of the original donor of a part of the land.

In 1925 it again became evident that the needs of the Hospital and University had outgrown their available funds. The Half-Century Fund Campaign was inaugurated and, again proving the loyalty of Baltimoreans to these two institutions, succeeded in collecting seven million dollars.

The total assets of the University today are not far from $35,000,000, and its scheme of building is nearing completion. Besides a vast number of original papers the Johns Hopkins publishes twenty serials; it liberally encourages investigation and research and maintains various fellowships to enable students of advanced standing to pursue their investigations. It has sent men of high standing into all corners of the earth, and has drawn to Baltimore for participation in the work of its staff, as lecturers or teachers besides those already mentioned, such men as, James Russell Lowell, in romance literature; William D. Whitney, in comparative philology; William James, in psychology; Sidney Lanier, in English literature; Charles S. Pierce, in logic; Alexander Graham Bell, in phonology; William K. Brooks, in biology; Simon Newcomb, in astronomy; Fabian Franklin, in mathematics; William T. Sedgwick, in biology.

Following in their footsteps are men who today are keeping the University in the front ranks of achievement. The students now number nearly 5000 men and women, and the service of the University to American education becomes yearly more significant.

As is true of the University, so it is also true of the Hospital, that it is not the buildings with their clinical institutes and dispensaries nor the great central Medical Library recently established in honor of Dr. Welch, with its 60,000 volumes; but it is the character of the men who have been connected with the Hospital in its early history, and those who are connected with it now, as well as men of note who have been graduated there and who hold important positions in institutions all over the world, who are responsible for the standing and achievement of the Johns Hopkins Hospital. By the men who have worked at this institution many fundamental facts have been discovered which have added to the sum total of medical knowledge.

The importance of this great Hospital to the community is attested by many available statistics, such as that the present book value of the Hospital and grounds is $4,334,917.75, and the actual value probably twice that amount; that starting in May of 1889 with 15 men on its staff and 272 beds, it now has 128 men on its staff and 620 beds.

It is gratifying to find that 50 per cent of the patients are treated free of cost, that 25 per cent pay a portion of the cost only, and that the Hospital is open to both white and colored patients from any portion of the United States.

To these facts may be added that the Hospital in 1927-8 admitted 582 white patients and 529 colored patients, that the wards took care of 1465 resident patients, and that 1100 babies had been born there.

It is an inspiring tribute to the generosity of private individuals that to the original buildings have been added the Phipps Clinic for psychiatric patients, the Marburg Ward for pay patients, both men and women, the Brady Urological Institute, the Harriet Lane Clinic for Children, the Wilmer Institute for the study and treatment of the eye, and a new Out-Patient and Diagnostic Building erected by the Carnegie Corporation.

It remains now only for the Hospital to erect a Medical and Surgical clinic in order to complete its original program of expansion, and the gift of $3,000,000 from an anonymous donor, announced in 1929 assures the completion of this project.

It is also to be noted that a splendid Social Service Department is responsible for all social problems and

The Johns Hopkins Hospital

follow-up work of non-resident patients; and that executive offices, a library, and a cafeteria are provided for its use.

But not to all these things must we look for the Hospital's real inspiration for service. It is primarily to the devotion and self-sacrifice of the men who built up this great organization, as well as to those who are carrying on at present, that we must look for the underlying foundations of achievement. Among these men it is at once Dr. William Osler, later Sir William Osler, its first Physician-in-Chief, that arrests the attention. Great qualities of both heart and mind made him a beacon light in the world of medicine. By Dr. William Osler, together with Dr. William Welch and Mr. Daniel Gilman, who acted as Director of the Hospital when its first opened, and Dr. Henry M. Hurd, its first Superintendent, the policy of the institution was shaped. To Dr. Osler is due the credit for the vision which foresaw that every doctor in the Hospital should also be a teacher, that bedside clinics were of inestimable value to the student doctor, and that qualities of the heart were as necessary to a successful physician as qualities of the mind. He made contacts in many ways with the city in which the Hospital is located, and was especially interested in its libraries. He invited the cooperation of physicians outside of the Hospital and of the country doctors of Maryland. He spoke and wrote continually of the sewage disposal of Baltimore, of the unsanitary conditions which existed at that time, and of their connection with typhoid fever and he played a large part in securing a new sewerage system for the city.

We are indebted to two men, Dr. Walter Reid and Dr. Lazear, at one time associated with the Johns Hopkins Hospital, who gave their lives to finding the cause of Yellow Fever. Dr. William Welch has spent years of his life in teaching preventive medicine. And to Dr. F. H. Baetjer we are indebted for much of the pioneer work done in the investigation of the X-ray.

Such men, and many others equally prominent, have shown the way not only to better hospital construction, more perfect hygienic conditions, and greater comfort for the sick, but they have set an example of unselfish devotion to the cause of medicine, without which imposing buildings, numbers of students, wards and medicines would count for but little.

It is through men of high caliber, of keen mind, and of good heart that the dreams of Johns Hopkins are being realized.

On the staff of the Rockefeller Institute are more Johns Hopkins graduates than those representing any other medical institution. The Director of the Rockefeller Institute is himself a Hopkins man, and so also is the head of its hospital. Four Hopkins men head departments in the new Henry Ford Hospital in Detroit. The Director of the Hospital of the University of Chicago is a Hopkins man, as also are the heads of the University Hospitals of Maryland and Georgia, of the Cornell Clinic of New York City, of the Barnes Hospital of St. Louis, of the Charles T.

SIR WILLIAM OSLER, REGIUS PROFESSOR OF MEDICINE AT OXFORD
UNIVERSITY AND FIRST PHYSICIAN-IN-CHIEF
OF THE JOHNS HOPKINS HOSPITAL
Copyright by Jeffres Studio. Used by permission

Miller Hospital of St. Paul, of the Hartford Hospital of Hartford, Connecticut, and of the Royal Mental Hospital of Glasgow, Scotland.

All of these men have come, either directly or indirectly, under the influence of Dr. William Osler, an outstanding man of the century. Only a great man can be simple, straightforward, honest, and fearless, and only a great man can speak as Dr. Osler did to his students. "I would urge you," he said, "to care more for the individual patient than for the special features of the disease. . . . To keep your own heart soft and tender. . . . Keep a looking-glass in your own heart, and the more carefully you scan your own frailties the more tender you are for those of your fellow-creatures. . . . In Charity we of the medical profession must live and move and have our being . . . . Cultivate peace of mind, serenity, the philosophy of Marcus Aurelius. Think not too much of tomorrow, but of the work of today, the work which is immediately before you. . . .

"A physician may possess the science of Harvey and the art of Sydenham and yet there may be lacking in him those finer qualities of heart and head which count for so much in life. . . . While doctors continue to practise medicine with their hearts as well as their heads, so long will there be a heavy balance in their favor in the bank of Heaven . . . . not a balance against which we can draw for bread and butter, or taxes or house-rent, but without which we should be poor indeed."

Osler has also said: "The whole art of medicine lies
in observation. . . . The student begins with the
patient, continues with the patient, and ends his studies
with the patient. Teach him how to observe, give
him plenty of facts to observe, and the lessons will
come out of the facts themselves."

How liberal a man was he who could say "In all ages
the prayer of Faith has healed the sick. . . . The
modern miracles at Lourdes and at Ste. Anne de
Beaupré in Quebec, and the wonder workings of the
so-called Christian Scientists are often genuine and
must be considered in discussing the foundations of
therapeutics. We physicians use the same power
every day. . . . Faith is a most precious com-
modity without which we should be very badly off."

This great man seldom revealed the innermost workings of his mind but gives us a glimpse of them in his
parting words to his fellow physicians in Baltimore
when leaving to assume the duties of Regius Professor
of Medicine in Oxford, to which position he had been
appointed by the Crown:

"I have three personal ideals. One, to do the day's
work well and not to bother about tomorrow. . . .
The second ideal has been to act the Golden Rule so far
as in me lay. . . . And the third has been to
cultivate such a measure of equanimity as would
enable me to bear success with humility, the affection
of my friends without pride, and to be ready when the
day of sorrow and grief came to meet it with the courage
befitting a man."

The Hopkins motto is, "If ye continue in my word, ye shall know the Truth; and the Truth shall make you free."

The highest aim of humanity is the search for Truth, and the greatest good which the endowments of Johns Hopkins are conferring upon mankind is to assist in this endeavor.

APPENDIX

"Baltimore, March 10th, 1873.

"To Francis T. King, President; and John W. Garrett, Hon. Geo. W. Dobbin, Galloway Cheston, Thomas M. Smith, Wm. Hopkins, Richard M. Janney, Joseph Merrefield, Francis White, Lewis N. Hopkins, Alan P. Smith, and Charles J. M. Gwinn, Trustees of 'The Johns Hopkins Hospital':

"Gentlemen:—

I have given you in your capacity of trustees, thirteen acres of land, situated in the city of Baltimore, and bounded by Wolfe, Monument, Broadway, and Jefferson streets, upon which I desire you to erect a hospital. It will be necessary to devote the present year to the grading of its surface to its proper drainage, to the laying out of the grounds, and the most careful and deliberate choice of a plan for the erection and arrangement of the new hospital buildings. It is my wish that the plan thus chosen shall be one which will permit symmetrical additions to the buildings which will be first constructed, in order that you may ultimately be able to receive four hundred patients, and that it shall provide for an hospital which shall in construction and arrangement compare favorably with any other institution of like character in this country or in Europe. It will therefore be your duty to obtain the advice and assistance of those at home or abroad who have achieved the greatest success in the construction and management of hospitals. I cannot press this injunction too strongly upon you, because the usefulness of this charity will greatly depend upon the plan which you may adopt for the construction and arrangement of the

87

buildings. It is my desire that you should complete this portion of your labor during the current year, and be in readiness to commence the building of the hospital in the spring of 1874.

"It will be your duty hereafter to provide for the erection upon other ground, of suitable buildings for the reception, maintenance and education of orphan colored children. I direct you to provide accomodation for three or four hundred children of this class; and you are also authorized to receive into this asylum, at your discretion, as belonging to such class, colored children who have lost one parent only, and in exceptional cases to receive colored children who are not orphans, but may be in such circumstancees as to require the aid of charity. I desire that you shall apply the yearly sum of twenty thousand dollars, or so much thereof as may be necessary, of the revenue of the property which you will hereafter receive, to the maintenance of the Orphan's Home intended for such children.

"In order to enable you to carry my wishes into full effect, I will now, and in each succeeding year during my life until the hospital buildings are fully completed and in readiness to receive patients, place at your disposal the sum of one hundred thousand dollars. In addition to the gift already made to you of the thirteen acres of land in the city of Baltimore upon which the hospital will be built, I have dedicated to its support and the payment of the annual sum provided to be paid for the support of the Orphans' Home, property which you may safely estimate as worth to-day two million of dollars, and from which your corporation will certainly receive a yearly revenue of one hundred and twenty thousand dollars, and which time and your diligent care will make more largely productive. If the Hospital and Orphans' Home are not built at my death, it will be your duty to apply the income arising from this property to their completion. When they are built, the income from the property will suffice for the maintenance. The indigent sick of this city and its environs, without regard to sex, age, or color, who require surgical or medical treatment, and who can be received into the hospital without peril to the other inmates, and the poor of the city and State, of all races, who are stricken down by any casualty, shall be received into the hospital without charge, for such periods of time and under such regulations as you may prescribe. It will be your duty to make such division of the sexes and patients among the several wards of the hospital as will best promote the actual usefulness of the charity. You will also provide for the reception of a limited number of patients who are able to make compensation for the room and attention they may require. The money received from such persons will enable you to appropriate a larger sum for for the relief of the sufferings of that class which I direct you to admit free of charge, and you will thus be enabled to afford to strangers, and to those of our own people who have no friends or relatives to care for them in sickness, and who are not objects of charity, the advantage of careful and skilful treatment.

"It will be your especial duty to secure for the service of the hospital, surgeons and physicians of the highest character and of the greatest skill. I desire you to establish, in connection with the hospital, a training school for female nurses. This provision will secure the services of women competent to care for the sick in the hospital wards, and will enable you to benefit the whole community by supplying it with a class of trained and experienced nurses.

"I wish the large grounds surrounding the hospital buildings to be properly enclosed by iron railings, and to be so laid out and planted with trees and flowers as to afford solace to the sick and be an ornament to the section of the city in which the grounds are located. I desire that you should, in due season, provide for a site and buildings of such description and at such distance from the city as your judgment shall approve, for the reception of convalescent patients. You will be able in this way to hasten the recovery of the sick, and to have always room in the main hospital building for other sick persons requiring immediate medical or surgical treatment. It is my special request that the influences of religion should be felt in and impressed upon the whole management of the hospital; but I desire, nevertheless, that the administration of the charity shall be undisturbed by sectarian influence, discipline, or control. In all your arrangements in relation to this hospital, you will bear constantly in mind that it is my wish and purpose that the institution should ultimately form a part of the medical school of that university for which I have made ample provision by my will. I have felt it to be my duty to bring these subjects to your particular attention, knowing that you will conform to the wishes which I definitely express. In other particulars I leave your board to the exercise of its discretion, believing that your good judgment and experience in life will enable you to make this charity a substantial benefit to the community.

"I am very respectfully your friend,
"Johns Hopkins."

II

The Last Will and Testament of Johns Hopkins

I, Johns Hopkins, of Baltimore County, in the State of Maryland, do make and publish this, my last Will and Testament, in manner and form following, that is to say:

First and principally, I commit, with humble reverence, my soul to the keeping of Almighty God.

I direct that all my debts and funeral expenses shall be paid by my Executors, herein after named.

I do give and devise into my friends, Francis White, Francis T. King and Charles J. M. Gwinn, and to the survivors or survivor of them, and to the heirs, executors and administrators of the survivor, the following pieces or parcels of property, situated in the City of Baltimore, belonging to me, namely, eight warehouses on the north side of Lombard street, between Light Street and Charles Street, and now known as Number Ninety-Six (96) Lombard Street, Number Ninety-Eight (98) Lombard Street, Number One Hundred (100) Lombard Street, Number One Hundred and two (102) Lombard Street, Number One Hundred and Four (104) Lombard Street, Number One Hundred and Six (106) Lombard Street, Number One Hundred and Eight (108) Lombard Street, and Number One Hundred and Ten (110) Lombard Street, and the warehouse on the southeast corner of Baltimore and Liberty Streets, now known as Number Two Hundred and Ninety-Seven Baltimore Street; with power to manage all affairs and concerns relating to the said property, or any of it, or the income arising therefrom, in such manner that the value and productiveness of the said property may be best maintained and enhanced.

In trust, nevertheless, for the children of my deceased brother, Samuel Hopkins, and for the benefit of James

Monroe Mercer, the husband of my niece Ella W. Mercer; in manner and form following, that is to say, in trust, to collect the rents, issues and profits thereof, and to apply the same, in the first place, to the payment of all charges and taxes upon, or repairs of, the said property, or any of it, and afterwards to pay, semi-annually, three-eighths parts of the clear rents, issues and profits thereof to my niece Ella W. Mercer, now wife of James Monroe Mercer, upon her separate receipt, for her separate use, free from the control of any husband she may now, or hereafter, have, for the period of her natural life; and, after the death of the said Ella W. Mercer, to apply so much of the said three-eighths parts of the said clear rents, issues and profits, as may be necessary, to the education and reasonable maintenance of any child, or children, of the said Ella W. Mercer, who may be living at her death, until the expiration of the period of twenty years after the death of the said Ella W. Mercer, at which period of time three-eighths parts of the said property so devised in trust for the children of my said deceased brother Samuel Hopkins and of James Monroe Mercer, together with any surplus of income, or property, proportionably arising therefrom, shall vest absolutely in the child, or children, of the said Ella W. Mercer, as tenants in common, the respective shares which their respective parents would have taken.

And upon the further trust to pay, semi-annually, one-eighth part of the clear rents, issues and profits thereof to James Monroe Mercer, the husband of my niece Ella W. Mercer, for the period of his natural life, and, after his death, to apply so much of the said one-eighth part of the said clear rents, issues and profits, as may be necessary, to the education and reasonable maintenance of any child, or children, of the said Ella W. Mercer, who may be living at his death, until the expiration of the period of twenty years after the death of the said Ella W. Mercer, at which period of time one-eighth part of the said property, so devised in trust for the children of my said deceased brother Samuel

Hopkins, and of James Monroe Mercer, together with any surplus of income, or property, proportionably arising therefrom, shall vest absolutely in the child, or children of the said Ella W. Mercer, as tenants in common, if there be more than one child; the issue of deceased children taking by substitution, as tenants in common, the respective shares which their respective parents would have taken.

And upon the further trust to pay, semi-annually, two-eighths parts of the clear rents, issues and profits thereof to my nephew, John J. Hopkins for the period of his natural life; and after the death of the said John J. Hopkins, to apply so much of the said two-eighths parts of the said clear rents, issues and profits as may be necessary to the education and reasonable maintenance of any child, or children, of the said John J. Hopkins, who may be living at his death, until the expiration of the period of twenty years after the death of the said John J. Hopkins, at which period of time two-eighths parts of the said property, so devised in trust for the children of my said deceased brother Samuel Hopkins, and of James Monroe Mercer, together with any surplus of income, or property proportionably arising therefrom, shall vest absolutely in the child, or children, of the said John J. Hopkins, as tenants in common, if there be more than one child; the issue of deceased children taking by substitution, as tenants in common, the respective shares which their respective parents would have taken.

And upon the further trust to pay, semi-annually, one-eighth part of the clear rents, issues, and profits thereof to my nephew, Mahlon Hopkins, for the period of his natural life; and, after the death of the said Mahlon Hopkins, to apply so much of the said one-eighth part of the said clear rents, issues, and profits as may be necessary, to the education and reasonable maintenance of any child, or children, of the said Mahlon Hopkins, who may be living at his death, until the expiration of the period of twenty years after the death of the said Mahlon Hopkins, at which period of time one-eighth part of the said property, so devised in trust for the children of my said deceased brother, Samuel Hopkins, and of James Monroe Mercer, together with any surplus of income, or property, proportionably arising therefrom, shall vest absolutely in the child or children of the said Mahlon Hopkins, as tenants in common, if there be more than one child; the issue of deceased children taking by substitution, as tenants in common, the respective shares which their respective parents would have taken.

And upon further trust to pay, semi-annually, one-eighth part of the clear rents, issues and profits thereof to my nephew Arundel Hopkins, for the period of his natural life; and after the death of the said Arundel Hopkins, to apply so much of the said one-eighth part of the said clear rents, issues and profits as may be necessary to the education and reasonable maintenance of any child, or children, of the said Arundel Hopkins, who may be living at his death, until the expiration of the period of twenty years after the death of the said Arundel Hopkins, at which period of time one-eighth part of the said property so devised in trust for the children of my deceased brother Samuel Hopkins, and of James Monroe Mercer, together with any surplus of income, or property, proportionably arising therefrom, shall vest absolutely in the child, or children, of the said Arundel Hopkins, as tenants in common, if there be more than one child: the issue of deceased children taking by substitution, as tenants in common, the respective shares which their respective parents would have taken.

I do give and devise into my friends Francis T. King, Francis White and Charles J. M. Gwinn, and to the survivors, or survivor of them, and to the heirs, executors, administrators and assigns of the survivor, the following pieces, or parcels of property, situate in the City of Baltimore, now belonging to me, namely four warehouses on the north side of Exchange Place, in the said city, now known as number fifty-four (54) Exchange Place, number fifty-six (56) Exchange Place, number fifty-eight (58) Exchange Place, and number sixty (60) Exchange Place, also six dwelling houses, with stores, on the north side of East Baltimore Street, in the said city, now known as number two (2) East Baltimore Street, number four (4) East Baltimore Street, number six (6) East Baltimore Street, number eight (8) East Baltimore Street, number ten (10) East Baltimore Street, and number twelve (12) East Baltimore Street, and two warehouses on the east side of Cheapside, now known as number twenty-nine (29) and twenty-nine and a half (29½), with power to manage and direct all affairs and concerns, relating to the said property, or any of it, in such manner that the value and productiveness of the said property may be best maintained and enhanced; in trust nevertheless, for the children of my sister, Sarah H. Janney, wife of Richard M. Janney; that is to say, in trust to collect the rents, issues and profits thereof, and to apply the same, in the first place to the payment of all charges and taxes upon, or repairs of the said property, or any of it, and afterwards to pay, semi-annually, one-fourth part of the clear rents, issues and profits thereof to my niece, Jane White now wife of Francis White, upon her separate receipt, for her separate use, free from the control of any husband she may now have or hereafter have, for the period of her natural life, and after the death of the said Jane White, to apply so much of the said one-fourth part of the said clear rents, issues and profits as may be necessary, to the education, and reasonable maintenance, in a proper manner, of any child, or children, of the said Jane White, who may be living at her death, until the expiration of the period of twenty years after the death of the said Jane White, at which period of time, one-fourth part of the said property, so devised in trust for the children of my said sister Sarah H. Janney, together with any surplus of income, or property, proportionably arising therefrom, shall vest absolutely in the child, or children of the said Jane White, as tenants in common, if there be more than one child; the issue of deceased children taking by substitution, as tenants in common, the respective shares which their respective parents would have taken.

And upon the further trust, to pay semi-annually, to my niece, Mrs. Margaret Elliott, wife of Joseph Elliott, of North Carolina, one-fourth part of the clear rents, issues and profits thereof, upon her separate receipt, for her separate use, free from the control of any husband she may now or hereafter have, for the period of her natural life; and after the death of the said Margaret Elliott, in trust to apply so much of the said one-fourth part of the said clear rents, issues and profits as may be necessary, to the education and reasonable maintenance, in a proper manner of any child or children of the said Margaret Elliott, who may be living at her death, until the expiration of the period of twenty years after the death of the said Margaret Elliott, at which period of time one-fourth part of the said property, so devised in trust for the children of my said sister, Margaret Elliott, together with any surplus of income, or property, proportionably arising therefrom, shall vest absolutely in the child or children of the said Margaret Elliott, as tenants in common, if there be more than one child; the issue of deceased children taking by substitution, as tenants in common, the respective shares which their respective parents would have taken.

And upon the further trust to pay, semi-annually, one-fourth part of the clear rents, issues and profits thereof, to my nephew, Samuel H. Janney, for the period of his natural life, and after the death of the said Samuel H. Janney, to apply so much of the said one-fourth part of the said clear rents, issues and profits as may be necessary to the education and reasonable maintenance of any child, or children, of the said Samuel H. Janney, at which period of time one-fourth part of the said property, so devised in trust for the children of my said sister, Sarah H. Janney, together with any surplus of income, or property, proportionably arising therefrom, shall vest absolutely in the child, or children, of the said Samuel H. Janney, as tenants in common, if there be more than one child; the issue of deceased children taking by substitution, as tenants in common, the respective share which their respective parents would have taken.

And upon the further trust to pay, semi-annually, one-fourth part of the clear rents, issues and profits thereof to my nephew, Johns Hopkins Janney for the period of his natural life, and after the death of the said Johns Hopkins Janney, to apply so much of the said one-fourth part of the said clear rents, issues and profits as may be necessary to the education and reasonable maintenance of any child, or children, of the said Johns Hopkins Janney, who may be living at his death, until the expiration of twenty years after the death of the said Johns Hopkins Janney, at which period of time one-fourth part of the said property, so devised in trust for the children of my said sister, Sarah H. Janney, together with any surplus of income, or property, propor-tionably arising therefrom, shall vest absolutely in the child, or children, of the said Johns Hopkins Janney, as tenants in common, if there be more than one child; the issue of de-ceased children taking by substitution, as tenants in common, the respective shares which their respective parents would have taken.

If any of the children of my deceased brother, Samuel Hopkins, or if my sister, Sarah H. Janney, should die without leaving any child, or children, or if any child, or children, of any one of the children of my said deceased brother, Samuel H. Janney, shall depart this life after the death of his, her, or their parent, (such parent being a child of my said deceased brother, Samuel Hopkins, or of my said sister, Sarah H. Janney), and before the expiration of the period of twenty years after the death of his, her, or their parent, (such being as, aforesaid, a child of my said brother Samuel Hopkins, or of my sister, Sarah H. Janney), then, and in such event, it is my will that the share, part, or interest of the child or children of my said deceased brother, Samuel Hopkins, or of my sister, Sarah H. Janney, so dying, and of the grand child, or grand children, of my said last mentioned brother or sister, so dying, shall be held by my said Trustees, and by the survivors of them, in trust, as to the realty, for the heirs at law of such deceased child, or grand child, or children, or grand children of my said brother, Samuel Hopkins, or of my said sister, Sarah H. Janney, and in trust, as to the personalty, for such person, or persons, as under the laws of this state would be entitled to be the distributees of the personal Estate of such deceased child, or grand child, children, or grand children; subject, however, in all respects, to the other limitations appointed by this, my last will and testament, in reference to the shares of the children of my said deceased brother, Samuel Hopkins, and of my sister, Sarah H. Janney, in so far as such limitations are applicable.

I give and devise to Samuel H. Congdon, of Maryland, Johns Hopkins Congdon, of Rhode Island, Elizabeth Congdon, of Rhode Island, and to Mary E. Wood, wife of William Wood, of New York, children of my sister, Mary R. Congdon, the following pieces, parcels of property, situate in the City of Baltimore, now belonging to me, to be by them held and enjoyed as tenants in common, and not as joint tenants; namely, five warehouses on the south side of Exchange Place, in said city, now known as number fifty-five (55) Exchange Place, number fifty-seven (57) Exchange Place, number fifty-nine (59) Exchange Place, number sixty-one (61) Exchange Place, and number sixty-three (63) Exchange Place.

I give unto Louis N. Hopkins, a son of my brother Joseph Hopkins, deceased, the double warehouse, now belonging to me, situated on the south side of Lombard street, in the city of Baltimore, now known as number one hundred and five (105) Lombard street.

I give and devise to Joseph Hopkins, a son of my brother, Joseph Hopkins, deceased, the double warehouse, now belonging to me, in the City of Baltimore, situated on the

North side of Lombard street, between Calvert street and Light street, now known as number eighty-eight and ninety (88 and 90) Lombard street; also two dwelling houses belonging to me, situated in the city aforesaid, known as numbers six and eight, (6 and 8) Wyeth street; also one dwelling house situated in the City aforesaid, known as number two hundred and sixty-five (265) Montgomery street; also one dwelling house, belonging to me, on Hughes street, in the rear of the dwelling house on Montgomery street, last above referred to.

I give and devise unto Gerard Hopkins and Samuel Hopkins, sons of my deceased brother Joseph Hopkins, as tenants in common, and not as joint tenants, the following lots and parcels of ground and property, situated in the City of Baltimore, and now belonging to me, to be equally divided between them; that is to say the thirty-six dwelling houses, fronting upon Sharp street, and upon West street, and upon Peach alley; being numbers three hundred and twenty-nine, (329), three hundred and thirty-one (331), three hundred and thirty-three, (333), three hundred and thirty-five (335), three hundred and thirty-seven, (337), three hundred and thirty-nine, (339), three hundred and forty-one, (341), three hundred and forty-three, (343), three hundred and forty-five, (345), three hundred and forty-seven, (347), three hundred and forty-nine, (349), three hundred and fifty-one, (351), three hundred and fifty-three, (353), three hundred and fifty-seven, (357), three hundred and fifty-nine, (359), three hundred and sixty-one, (361), and three hundred and sixty-three, (363), Sharp street; and being numbers two hundred and fifty-one, (251), two hundred and fifty-three, (253), two hundred and fifty-five, (255), two hundred and fifty-seven, (257), two hundred and fifty-nine, (259), two hundred and sixty-one, (261), and two hundred and sixty-three, (263), West street; and being number one hundred and one, (101), one hundred and three, (103), one hundred and five, (105), one hundred and seven, (107), one hundred and nine, (109), one hundred and eleven, (111), one hundred and thirteen, (113), one hundred and fifteen, (115), one hundred and seventeen, (117), and one hundred and nineteen, (119) Peach alley; also six dwelling houses belonging to me, on the east of Plum alley, between Montgomery and Henrietta streets; also the dwelling house known as number one hundred and twenty-eight, (128), on the west side of Sharp street; and the dwelling house known as number forty-eight (48), on the south side of Conway street; all situated, as aforesaid, in the City of Baltimore.

I give and devise the dwelling house, on Saratoga street, in the City of Baltimore, wherein I reside in winter, to my sister, Eliza H. Crenshaw, during her natural life.

I give and bequeath the furniture, silver-plate, wines and household articles, in said dwelling house, and my carriage and horses, to my said sister, Eliza H. Crenshaw, absolutely.

I direct that my said dwelling house shall, during the life of my sister, be kept insured to an amount sufficient to prevent serious loss, by the Trustees of "The Johns Hopkins Hospital," hereinafter named, at the cost of the said "The Johns Hopkins Hospital."

In order to provide a sufficient fund for the support of my said sister, Eliza H. Crenshaw, I bequeath unto my executors, hereinafter named, and the survivors, or survivor of them, the sum of one hundred thousand dollars in the Bonds of the Pittsburgh and Connellsville Railroad Company now in my possession in trust, to pay the interest accruing thereon, from the date of my death, apportioning the same for that purpose, to the said Eliza H. Crenshaw, during her natural life.   After the death of my said sister, Eliza H. Crenshaw, I give and devise my said dwelling house on Saratoga street to "The Johns Hopkins Hospital," a Corporation hereinafter particularly referred to, for its corporate uses; and immediately upon the death of my said sister, Eliza H. Crenshaw, I direct my said executors and the survivors, or survivor of them, to deliver up, assign and transfer the one hundred thousand dollars of the bonds of the Pittsburgh and Connellsville Railroad Company aforesaid, bequeathed in trust as aforesaid, to the said, "The Johns Hopkins Hospital" for its corporate uses.

I give and bequeath unto my brother-in-law, Richard M. Janney, the sum of ten thousand dollars.

I give and devise to my sister, Sarah H. Janney, wife of Richard M. Janney, the sum of five thousand dollars.

I give and bequeath unto my sister, Margaret White, wife of Miles White, the sum of five thousand dollars.

I give and bequeath unto Elizabeth S. Hopkins, the widow of my brother, Joseph Hopkins, the sum of five thousand dollars.

I give and bequeath unto Lavinia Hopkins, the wife of my brother, Samuel Hopkins, the sum of five thousand dollars.

I give and bequeath unto the children of Ezekiel Hopkins, of Cecil County, Maryland, the sum of five thousand dollars, to be divided equally among them, share and share alike.

I give and bequeath unto the children of my cousin, Isaiah Hopkins, the sum of five thousand dollars, to be divided between or among them, share and share alike.

I give and bequeath to the two unmarried daughters of Gerard Hopkins (of Joseph,) to be divided between them, share and share alike, the sum of two thousand dollars.

I give and bequeath unto Elizabeth Hopkins, widow of Basil Hopkins, the sum of five thousand dollars.

I give and bequeath unto my friend, John J. Barry, the sum of four thousand dollars.

I give and bequeath unto my servant man, James, the house in which he now resides, on French street, in the City of Baltimore, and the sum of five thousand dollars.

I give and bequeath to my servant woman, Chloe, the sum of one thousand dollars.

I give and bequeath to my servant man, Charles, the sum of two thousand dollars.

I give and bequeath unto "The Baltimore Manual Labor

School for Indigent Boys" the sum of twenty thousand dollars.

I give and bequeath unto the Maryland Institute for the Promotion of the Mechanic Arts, for the use of its School of Design, the sum of ten thousand dollars.

I give and bequeath unto the "Home of the Friendless" the sum of ten thousand dollars.

I give and bequeath unto the Baltimore Orphan Asylum, referred to in the Act of Assembly of the State of Maryland of December Session, 1849, chapter 32, the sum of ten thousand dollars.

I give, devise and bequeath unto "The Johns Hopkins University," a corporation formed at my instance, under the laws of Maryland, by certificate duly recorded among the Records of Baltimore County, my country place known as "Clifton," containing about three hundred and thirty acres, and all the shares of the capital stock of the Baltimore and Ohio Railroad Company, whereof I shall die possessed, (except the stock known as preferred stock of said Company, upon which a dividend of six per centum and no more is payable by said Company,) and I recommend the said "The Johns Hopkins University" not to dispose of the said capital stock, or of the stock, accruing thereon by way of increment, or dividend, but to keep the said stock and said increment, or dividend stock, if any, as an investment; and I direct that the buildings, necessary for the purposes of the said "The Johns Hopkins University," shall be constructed out of the money dividends as they accrue on said stock; and that the said University and the trustees should maintain the said University, afterwards, out of its receipts from scholars, and out of the annual revenue derived from the devise and bequest hereby made, without encroaching upon the principal fund. And I further enjoin upon the said University, and the trustees thereof, the duty of voting and representing the said stock with diligence, zeal and perfect fidelity to the trust I have reposed in them, especially desiring that each and every trustee thereof will abstain from all action which may tend to subordinate the Baltimore and Ohio Railroad Company to any political influence, or management, and will at all times, use his or their influence or power with the purpose of promoting its usefulness, and the value of the stock of that company, which I have hereby bequeathed.

And I further request the trustees of the said University to establish, from time to time, such number of free scholarships in the said University as may be judicious; and to distribute the said scholarships amongst such candidates from the States of Maryland, Virginia, and North Carolina, as may be most deserving of choice, because of their character and intellectual promise; and to educate the young men so chosen free of charge.

I give, devise and bequeath unto "The Johns Hopkins Hospital" a corporation formed at my instance, under the laws of Maryland, by Certificate recorded among the Records of Baltimore city, all the real and leasehold estate, not hereinbefore specifically disposed of, and wheresoever the same may be situate, of which I may die seized, or possessed, and also all the Bank stocks, owned by me, at my death, in Banks located, or doing business within, or beyond the limits of this State, to be held, used and applied by the said "The Johns Hopkins Hospital" in and for and to its corporate purposes, in accordance with the provisions of its existing Certificate or Charter of Incorporation, or with the provisions of such Act, or Acts of Assembly, amending its Certificate or Charter of Incorporation, as the trustees thereof, acting upon my recommendations hereinafter made, may see fit to procure to be passed and accepted.

And as I am of the opinion that the ward, or building, to be under the control of the said Hospital, which is to be erected for the reception and care of colored orphan children, ought also to be opened for the reception and proper training of destitute colored children, and that said ward ought, moreover, to be separated wholly, and built at a distance from, the wards, or buildings intended for sick poor white persons, or of sick poor colored persons; and also for authority to receive and care for destitute colored children, in such building, erected for the reception and care of orphan colored children; but it shall be the duty of the said trustees of the said "The Johns Hopkins Hospital" to supervise the concerns, interests and wants of all the several wards, or sub-divisions, of the said "The Johns Hopkins Hospital" wherever the said wards, or subdivisions, may be located, in such manner that the interests and wants of each of said subdivisions, or wards, may be fully and impartially protected and promoted.

And I desire that the said trustees of the said "The Johns Hopkins Hospital" shall make ample provision out of the property, real and personal by this my last will and testament devised and bequeathed to the said "The Johns Hopkins Hospital," not only for the ward, or building, intended for the use of sick poor white persons, and for the use of sick poor colored persons, and for the care of such inmates, but for the ward, or building intended for the reception and care of colored orphan and destitute children, as aforesaid.

I give, devise and bequeath all the rest, residue and remainder, of the estate of which I shall be seized, or possessed, at my death of whatsoever nature and description the same may be which has not been disposed of by this my last will and testament, or so much thereof as I shall not hereafter dispose of by my codicil, or codicils made hereto, or by gift, or gifts, or in any other manner in my life time, unto such persons of my kindred as would be entitled to such rest, residue and remainder of my estate, if such rest, residue and remainder had constituted my whole estate, and I had departed this life intestate.

Although I have full confidence in the affection of my kindred, and believe that it would be the pleasure of each one of them to promote the objects, to which I have by this my last will and testament dedicated the greater portion of my

fortune, yet, nevertheless, in the exercise of ordinary pru-
dence, it is my duty to guard fully against the effects of any
evil counsel or influence, which may seek to disturb any of
the provisions of this my last will, therefore I do further
direct, and declare, that if any person named in this my last
will and testament, and to whom, or for whose use, I have
made any devise, or bequest, or any person claiming through,
under, or in trust for such person, shall, at any time, during
the life of such person, or within twenty-one years after the
death of said person, dispute the validity of this my last will,
or of any of the dispositions herein, or in any codicil hereto,
contained, or shall at any time, during such period as aforesaid, refuse to confirm this my will, or any codicil hereto
so far as he, she, or they lawfully can, or to do such acts and
things, as of him, her, or them can be reasonably demanded
for giving full effect to all, or any of such dispositions, or if
any proceeding, whatever, shall, at any time, during such
period as aforesaid, be taken with the consent, or connivance
of any such person, or persons, as aforesaid, by means, or in
consequence of which, any estate, or interest could be in any
way attainable by such person, or persons, as aforesaid, of
larger extent, or value, than is or shall be by this my will,
or any codicil hereto, given to the said person or persons, and
such proceeding shall not be formally and at once disavowed,
stayed, or resisted by the said person, or persons as aforesaid,
to the full extent of his or their power and ability so to do,
then and in such case, all the dispositions herein, or in any
codicil hereto contained, in favor of the said person, or persons shall cease, and be void to all intents and purposes
whatsoever, and are hereby revoked accordingly. And in
the event lastly hereinbefore contemplated, as to all the real,
leasehold, and personal estate so forfeited as aforesaid, I give
and devise the same to "The Johns Hopkins Hospital" incorporated at my instance as aforesaid, under the laws of
Maryland, to be by it applied to its proper corporate uses.

I further direct that no claim shall be made by my executors, or the survivors, or survivor of them, or by any person claiming under me, against any nephew or niece who may be named as a devisee or legatee in this my last will and testament, or who may be entitled to receive any benefit or advantage as a cestui qui trust under this my last will and testament, for or by reason of any debt due by such person to me, although such indebtedness may appear upon my books, or by vouchers or evidence of debt in my possession, except where such claim may exist by reason of the non-payment by such devisee or legatee of commercial paper, which has not become due at the time of my death, for I do hereby forgive all and every debt due to me by any nephew or niece named, or referred to in this my last will and testament, except as above provided for, intending, except as so provided for, that every devise or bequest made by me to, or in favor of any such niece or nephew so indebted to me, should be enjoyed in the same manner and to as full an extent as if no debt were due to me by or from such niece or nephew.

I further direct my executors to pay all commercial paper endorsed by me, and which remains unpaid by the party or parties primarily responsible thereon, without delay, when proof of such claims against my estate is made according to law.

I further declare and provide that, in case any devise, legacy, or bequest in this my last will and testament should fail to take effect, for any reason whatsoever, then, and in such event, I give, devise and bequeath the said property, real, leasehold or personal, or of whatsoever nature it may be intended by this my last will and testament to have been devised, given or bequeathed, and which said devise, legacy or bequest may fail to take effect, for any reason whatsoever as aforesaid, to "The Johns Hopkins Hospital" for its corporate purposes.

I further declare that in the several devises and bequests of real, leasehold and personal estate, by me hereinbefore made, it has not been my purpose or intention that any charges, or incumbrances, existing at my death on any such real, leasehold or personal estate, should be paid out of my other real or personal estate; but it is my purpose and intention that every devisee, or legatee, or cestui qui use, or cestui qui trust named, or referred to in this my last will and testament, should take and receive the real, leasehold or personal estate so devised or bequeathed, or the benefit thereof, charged with and subject to any charge, or charges, incumbrance, or incumbrances, existing thereon, and be bound to assume the payment, performance or satisfaction of the same, and that my other real and personal estate should be exonerated therefrom.

I empower my executors, hereinafter named, to compound, or to allow time, or to accept security, real or personal, for any debt, or debts owing to my estate, and to adjust by arbitration, or otherwise, disputes in relation thereto, or in relation to debts, or demands, against my estate.

I do further give to the several trustees named in this my last will and testament, and to their successors in the said trust, and to my executors, and to the survivor or survivors of them, and to the executors, administrators and assigns of the survivor, all powers which may be necessary for the preservation, direction, repair, management, or profitable use of any property, real or personal, devised or bequeathed by me and remaining from time to time under their, or his government, or control, until such time as their respective duties, and the duties of each one of them in relation to the said trusts and property, shall be fully performed.

And I further declare that the several trustees appointed by this my last will and testament, and to the heirs, executors, administrators and assigns of them, and of each and every of them, shall be charged and chargeable respectively for such monies only as they respectively, shall actually receive by virtue of the trusts hereby in them reposed.

And I do hereby revoke all other testamentary dispositions by me heretofore made, declaring this and none other to be my last will and testament.

I do appoint my friends, Francis White, of Baltimore County, Francis T. King, of Baltimore City, and Charles J. M. Gwinn, of Baltimore City, now temporarily residing in Baltimore County, who are hereinbefore named as Trustees for certain purposes, to be also Executors of this my last Will and Testament; and I do give and bequeath to them the sum of thirty thousand dollars, to be divided equally among them; and I declare that the said legacy, so given, is in lieu and in place of all commissions which might accrue to all and each of them as Executors, or Executor, under this my last Will and Testament, and shall be by each of them agreed to be so received, and that such agreement of each of said persons shall be evidenced by the assent of each to act as such Executor. And I further declare that in case any one or more of my said Executors should depart this life before my death, then and in that event I appoint my nephew Lewis N. Hopkins to be an Executor of, and Trustee under, this my last Will and Testament, in the room and place of that one of my said Executors and Trustees, who may so first depart this life; and I do appoint my cousin, William Hopkins, son of Gerard T. Hopkins, deceased, to be an Executor and Trustee under this my last Will and Testament, in the room and place of that one of my said Executors and Trustees who may next afterwards depart this life; and I declare that all the trusts, powers and discretions, and all the restrictions and obligations, which are hereby vested in, or imposed upon, my Executors herein named, may be executed by and shall be held to be binding upon the said Lewis N. Hopkins, or William Hopkins, and upon both of them, upon his or their acceptance of the said office and trust or trusts, in the same manner and to the same extent as if he or they had been originally named as Executor or Executors, and as Trustee or Trustees, in this my last Will and Testament; and I direct and empower the Trustees, or the survivors or survivor of them, named in this my last Will and Testament, to fill up any vacancies which from time to time shall occur in the trusteeship aforesaid after my death by the choice of my nephew Lewis N. Hopkins, and William Hopkins, son of Gerard T. Hopkins, in the order in which they are here named, to fill such vacancies as they occur, and all the trusts, powers and discretions by this my last Will and Testament vested in my said Trustees, herein named, may be executed by the Trustees for the time being of my Will.

In testimony whereof I have hereunto set my hand and affixed my seal this ninth day of July, in the year eighteen hundred and seventy.

JOHNS HOPKINS, (SEAL)

Signed, sealed, published and declared by the above named Johns Hopkins as and for his last Will and Testament, in our presence, who at his request, in his presence, and in the presence of each other, have hereto set our hands as witnesses hereto.

James Hooper,
James B. Edwards,
David A. Jones,
Chas. G. Kerr.

BALTIMORE COUNTY, SS.

On this 27th day of December, 1873, came James Hooper, David A. Jones and Charles G. Kerr, subscribing witnesses, to the aforegoing Last Will and Testament of Johns Hopkins, late of said County, deceased, and made oath on the Holy Evangely of Almighty God, that they did see the Testator sign and seal this Will, that they heard him publish, pronounce and declare the same to be his Last Will and Testament; that at the time of his so doing he was to the best of their apprehension of sound and disposing mind, memory and understanding, and that they together with James B. Edwards, who is now deceased, subscribed their names as witnesses to this Will in his presence at his request, and in the presence of each other.

Test:

Jos. B. MITCHELL,
Register of Wills for Baltimore County.

MARYLAND:

Baltimore County, Sct:

I hereby certify that the aforegoing is a true copy of the Original Will of Johns Hopkins, late of Baltimore County, on the 27th day of December, A.D. 1873.

SEAL   In testimony whereof, I hereunto set my hand and affix the seal of my office, this 27th day of December, A.D. 1873.

Jos. B. MITCHELL,
Register of Wills for Baltimore County.

FIRST CODICIL

I, Johns Hopkins, of Baltimore county, in the State of Maryland, having heretofore made my last Will and Testament, dated on the ninth day of July, in the year eighteen hundred and seventy, do now make this Codicil to my said last Will and Testament, in manner and form as follows, that is to say:

Inasmuch as I have determined to increase the amount of the property, devised in trust in my said last Will and Testament for the benefit of the children of my deceased brother, Samuel Hopkins and of James Monroe Mercer, and also to increase the amount of the property devised in trust, in my said last Will and Testament for the benefit of the children of my sister, Sarah H. Janney, to the extent and in the manner hereinafter shown by this Codicil, now, therefore in order

to give effect to my said purposes, I do give and devise unto
my friends Francis White, Francis T. King, and Charles
J. M. Gwinn, and to the survivors and survivor of them,
and to the heirs, executors and administrators of the survivor, the warehouse now known as number one hundred
and fifty-two (152) West Pratt street, in the city of Baltimore, and also the two warehouses on the east side of South
Frederick street, at the south-east corner of Frederick and
Second streets, in the city of Baltimore, known and designated as numbers nineteen (19) twenty-one (21) twenty-
three (23) and twenty-five (25) South Frederick street, in
trust, nevertheless, for the children of my deceased brother
Samuel Hopkins, and for the benefit of James Monroe
Mercer, the husband of my niece, Ella W. Mercer, in manner
and form following, that is to say, in trust to hold the same,
and to collect and apply the rents, issues and profits thereof
in the same manner, as if the said property mentioned by
me as aforesaid in this clause of this Codicil, had formed and
constituted a portion of the pieces, or parcels of property,
by me set apart in my said last Will and Testament in trust
for the children of my said deceased brother, Samuel Hopkins, and for the benefit of the said James Monroe Mercer;
and I do further declare that every provision and limitation
made in my said last Will and Testament in relation to the
property therein and thereby devised in trust for the children
of my said deceased brother, Samuel Hopkins, and for the
benefit of James Monroe Mercer aforesaid, shall be held,
considered and taken as applying to the property devised
by this clause of this Codicil, in the same manner and to as
large an extent, in every particular, as if the said property
devised by this Codicil, had originally formed a part of the
property devised by my said last Will and Testament in
trust for the children of my deceased brother, Samuel Hopkins, and for the benefit of James Monroe Mercer aforesaid.

I do further give and devise unto my friends Francis

White, Francis T. King and Charles J. M. Gwinn, and to the survivors and survivor of them, and to the heirs, executors and administrators of the survivor, the warehouse known and designated as number one hundred and fifty (150) West Pratt street, situated at the north-east corner of Pratt and Hollingsworth streets, in the city of Baltimore, and also the warehouse adjoining said last named warehouse on the eastern side thereof, and also the three warehouses situated on the east side of Hollingsworth street, in the city of Baltimore, in the rear of the said warehouse above referred to, and designated by the number one hundred and fifty (150) West Pratt street, and adjoining the rear of said last named warehouse, or separated therefrom by an alley-way only, in trust, nevertheless, for the children of my sister, Sarah H. Janney, in manner and form following, that is to say, in trust to hold the same and to collect and apply the rents, issues and profits thereof, as if the said several pieces of property so by me mentioned as aforesaid, in this clause of this Codicil, had formed and constituted portions of the pieces or parcels of property by me set apart in my said last Will and Testament, in trust for the children of my sister, Sarah H. Janney, wife of Richard M. Janney, and I do further declare that every provision and limitation made in my said last Will and Testament in relation to the property therein and thereby devised in trust for the children of my said sister, Sarah H. Janney, shall be held, considered and taken as applying to the property devised by this clause of this Codicil, in the same manner and to as large an extent in every particular, as if the said property devised by this Codicil, had originally formed a part of the property devised by my said last Will and Testament in trust for the children of my said sister, Sarah H. Janney.

I do further declare that it is my wish that the trustees of "The Johns Hopkins Hospital" shall apply to the Legislature of Maryland for such additional authority as they may require to enable them to educate the orphan and destitute colored children by them received into their charge, and shall use and employ such portion of the net income of the property (not exceeding one-fourth part thereof however) devised and bequeathed to them by me, as may be necessary to enable them to perform the duty of receiving, caring for and educating such orphan and destitute colored children, and I do further direct that, when such authority is obtained, the said trustees shall expend such portion of the said one-fourth part of said income as may be necessary in the reception, care and education of said orphan and destitute colored children.

And I also declare it to be my wish that my said trustees shall also apply for such additional authority as they may require, to enable them to provide proper and respectable employment for such orphan and destitute colored children so by them received and cared for, when such children shall arrive at a suitable age.

Whereas, since the execution of my said last will and testament, I have made considerable investments in real and leasehold estate, and may make other purchases thereof, and have suffered losses of large sums of money in business transactions, and may encounter others of like nature;

And Whereas, also I have determined that the legacies and bequests, by me made in my said last will and testament, shall not be reduced because of said investments and losses, or because of other investments or losses to be by me made, or incurred, but that the said legacies and bequests may fully take effect, and may be subject only to the particular charges existing upon the same, as aforesaid, at the time of my death, I do hereby expressly charge any sum, in which my personal estate may be deficient, for the payment of said legacies and bequests, and in which it may be deficient for the payment of debts not charged upon or secured by specific real or personal property, by me bequeathed or devised, in equal parts, upon the estate, real and personal, by me devised and bequeathed, by my said last will and testament, and by this codicil, to "The Johns Hopkins Hospital," and upon the estate real and personal, by me devised and bequeathed by my last will and testament, and by this codicil, to "The Johns Hopkins University." It being my will and intention that one-half part of said deficiency, if any, should be paid by the said "The Johns Hopkins Hospital," and one-half part of said deficiency should be paid by the said "The Johns Hopkins University."

And Whereas, by my said last will and testament, I did give, devise and bequeath all the rest, residue and remainder of the estate of which I might be seized, or possessed, at my death, and which was not otherwise disposed of by my said last will and testament or by any codicil or codicils made thereto, or by gift or otherwise, in my life time, unto such persons of my kindred as would be entitled to such rest, residue and remainder of my estate, if such rest, residue and remainder had constituted my whole estate, and I had departed this life intestate.

And Whereas, upon due consideration, believing that my said kindred have been otherwise sufficiently provided for by my said last will and testament and by this codicil, I have determined to dispose otherwise of the said rest, residue and remainder of my real and personal estate.

Now I do hereby revoke the said devise and bequest so made of all the rest, residue and remainder of my estate, and I do hereby give, devise and bequeath all the said rest, residue and remainder of the estate, real and personal, of which I shall be seized, or possessed at my death, of whatsoever nature and description the same may be, to "The Johns Hopkins University" and to "The Johns Hopkins Hospital" as tenants in common, and not as joint tenants, to be equally divided between them, share and share alike; the share of each corporation in the said rest, residue and remainder of my real and personal estate to be held, used and applied by such corporation in, for and to its corporate purposes, in accordance with the provisions of its existing certificate, or charter of incorporation, or with the provisions of such Act or Acts of Assembly amending its certificate or charter of incorporation as the trustees thereof may procure to be passed and accepted.

Inasmuch as I deem it to be my duty to protect the dispositions made by me of my estate by my last will and testament, and by this Codicil, in the most formal, strict and solemn manner, in which I can protect the same, I do, therefore, in order that my wishes may be fully respected, again declare that if any person named in my said last will and testament, and to whom, or for whose use, I have made any devise, or bequest or provision or any person claiming through, under, or in trust for such person, shall at any time during the life of such person, or within twenty-one years after the death of such person, dispute the validity of my Last Will and Testament, or of any of the dispositions made in my said Last Will and Testament, or in this Codicil, or in any Codicil to be hereafter made to said Last Will and Testament, or shall at any time, during such period as aforesaid, refuse to confirm my last will and testament, or this Codicil, or any Codicil hereafter made to said last will and testament, or refuse to confirm any disposition, devise, or bequest of property made thereby, so far as he, she, or they lawfully can, or to do such acts, and things as of him, her, or them can be reasonably demanded for giving full effect to all, or any of such dispositions, devises, or bequests; or if any proceeding, whatever, shall at any time during such period as aforesaid, be taken with the consent, or connivance, of any such person or persons, as aforesaid, by means, or in consequence of which, any estate or interest could be in any way attainable by such person or persons as aforesaid, of larger extent, or value than is, or shall be by my said last will and testament, or by this Codicil, or by any Codicil hereafter made to said last will and testament, given to the said person or persons and such proceeding shall not be formally and at once disavowed, stayed, or resisted by the said person, or persons as aforesaid, to the full extent of his, or their, power and ability so to do, then and in such case, all the dispositions, made in my said last will and testament, or in this Codicil, or in any Codicil, to be hereafter made to my said last will and testament, in favor of the said person or persons, shall cease and be void to all intents and purposes whatsoever, and are hereby revoked accordingly.

And in the event lastly hereinbefore contemplated, as to all the real, leasehold and personal estate, so forfeited as aforesaid, I give and devise the same to "The Johns Hopkins Hospital" and to "The Johns Hopkins University" as tenants in common, and not as joint tenants, to be equally divided between them, share and share alike; the share of each corporation in the property so acquired to be held, used and applied by such corporation in, for and to its corporate purposes, in accordance with the provisions of its existing certificate, or charter of incorporation, as the Trustees thereof may procure to be passed and accepted.

Finally in all other respects, I do confirm my said last will and testament.

In testimony whereof, I have hereunto set my hand and affixed my seal this thirty-first day of October, in the year eighteen hundred and seventy-one.

JOHNS HOPKINS. (SEAL)

Signed, sealed, published and declared by the above named Johns Hopkins, as and for a Codicil to his last Will and Testament, in our presence, who at his request, in his presence and in the presence of each other, have hereunto set our hands as witnesses hereto.

David A. Jones,
William P. Ingle,
John A. Compton.
Baltimore County, Ss:

On this 27th day of December, 1873, came David A. Jones, William P. Ingle and John A. Compton, subscribing witnesses to the aforegoing Codicil to the Last Will and Testament of Johns Hopkins, late of said County, deceased, and made oath on the Holy Evangely of Almighty God, that they did see the Testator sign and seal this Codicil, that they heard him publish, pronounce, and declare the same to be a Codicil to his Last Will and Testament; that at the time of his so doing he was to the best of their apprehension of sound and disposing mind, memory and understanding, and that they subscribed their names as witnesses to this Codicil in his presence at his request, and in the presence of each other.

Sworn to in Open Court,

Test; Jos. B. Mitchell,

Register of Wills for Baltimore County.

In testimony that the aforegoing is a true copy taken from the original filed and of record in the Office of the Register of Wills for Baltimore County.

SEAL   I hereunto subscribe my name and affix the seal of my office, this 27th day of December, A.D. 1873.

Test: Jos. B. Mitchell,

Register of Wills for Baltimore County.

SECOND CODICIL

I, Johns Hopkins, of Baltimore County, in the State of Maryland, do make this Codicil, to the last Will and Testament by me heretofore executed.

I give, devise and bequeath to Samuel Hopkins and Gerard Hopkins of Howard County, in this State, and to the survivor of them, and to the heirs and assigns of the survivor, all the estate and property heretofore by me devised, or bequeathed to my nephew Lewis N. Hopkins; and also the warehouse formerly occupied by Hopkins Brothers & Company, in the prosecution of their business, which said warehouse is in the rear of the warehouse which was by my last will specifically devised to the said Lewis N. Hopkins, in trust, nevertheless to receive the rents, issues and profits of all of said property and to pay the net income therefrom, after deducting the necessary expenses attending the management of said property, to my said nephew, Lewis N. Hopkins, during his natural life, and, after his death, in trust to hold the said property and the rents, issues and profits thereof in trust for any child, or children of the said Lewis N. Hopkins, the said children, if there be more than one child, to be entitled to share equally therein.

I do further hereby expressly release my nephew Lewis N. Hopkins and my nephew Johns Hopkins Janney, partners now trading under the name and firm of Hopkins & Janney, and each of them, from all liability to pay any debt, or debts due by them, as a firm, or which may become due by them as a firm to me, or to my estate by reason of transactions originating in my lifetime, to the extent of sixty thousand dollars of said indebtedness, but to no greater or other extent.

And whereas, I have heretofore executed a certain emorandum in writing and delivered the same to Sarah H. Janney, in which I endeavored in a time of sickness, and not, perhaps in due form of law, to give and devise certain lots belonging to me at the Fair Grounds and a lot formerly belonging to E. Thomas, to Johns Hopkins Janney, my nephew, now I do hereby expressly refer to the said memorandum and devise the particular lots belonging to me at the Fair Grounds and the lot formerly belonging to the said E. Thomas, but now belonging to me, to the said Johns Hopkins Janney.

And in other respects I do confirm my said will and any codicil thereto heretofore made, imposing upon my executors and trustees the duty of enforcing each and every provision of my said last will, or of my codicil thereto to the utmost of their powers. In witness whereof I hereto set my hand and seal on this thirteenth day of December, in the year eighteen hundred and seventy-three.

JOHNS HOPKINS. (SEAL)

Signed, sealed published and declared by the above named Johns Hopkins, as and for a codicil to his last will and testament, in our presence, who, at his request, in his presence and in the presence of each other, have hereunto set our hands as witnesses hereto.

N. R. Smith,
A. S. Abell,
George V. Longcope.

Baltimore County, Ss:

On this 29th day of December, 1873, came N. R. Smith, A. S. Abell and G. V. S. Longcope, subscribing witnesses to the aforegoing Codicil to the last Will and Testament of Johns Hopkins, late of said County, deceased, and made oath on the Holy Evangely of Almighty God, that they did see the Testator sign and seal this Codicil, that they heard him publish, pronounce, and declare the same to be a second Codicil to his Last Will and Testament; that at the time of his so doing he was to the best of their apprehension of sound and disposing mind, memory and understanding, and that they subscribed their names as witnesses to this Codicil in his presence at his request, and in the presence of each other.

Test: Joseph B. Mitchell,
Register of Wills for Baltimore County.

Baltimore County, Ss:

On the 27th day of December, 1873, came Charles J. M. Gwinn and made oath on the Holy Evangely of Almighty God, that he does not know of any other Will or Codicil of Johns Hopkins late of said County, deceased, other than the above Instruments of Writing, and that he found the same at the Merchant's National Bank of Baltimore, on or about the 24th day of December, 1873.

Sworn to in Open Court,

Test: Jos. B. Mitchell,
Register of Wills for Baltimore County.

In testimony that the aforegoing is a true copy taken from the original filed and of record in the Orphans' Court of Baltimore, County.

SEAL   I hereunto subscribe my name and affix the seal of my office, this 27th day of December A.D. 1873.

Test: Jos. B. Mitchell,
Register of Wills for Baltimore County.

III

THE HOPKINS GENEALOGY

WILLIAM HOPKINS

The first Hopkins mentioned as living in Anne Arundel County. He owned Hopkins Plantation at Greenberry's Point, and was among the "Men of Severn" in 1657.

GERARD (or Garrard) HOPKINS

Of Anne Arundel County. He made his will in 1691 and called himself "Planter." He was a brother of William Hopkins, preceding. Married——Thomsin

Issue:
Garrard
Ann
Thomson
Mary

GARRARD (or Gerard) HOPKINS

Of Anne Arundel County. Married, 1700–1, Margaret Johns

Issue:
Margaret
Elizabeth
Joseph
Gerard
Philip
Samuel

Richard
William
Johns

JOHNS HOPKINS   Married (third) February
                                 16,   1758,   Elizabeth
                                 Thomas

Issue:
Samuel, born February 3, 1759.
Philip
Richard
Mary
Margaret
Gerard T.
Elizabeth
Evan
Ann
Rachel
William

SAMUEL HOPKINS   Died December 9, 1814.
                                 Married, 1792, Hannah
                                 Janney

Issue:
Joseph Janney
JOHNS—born May 19, 1795—died December 24, 1873
Eliza
Sarah
Hannah
Samuel
Mahlon
Philip
Margaret
Gerard
Mary

See *The Thomas Book* by Lawrence Buckley Thomas, D.D.
1896, Henry T. Thomas Co., N. Y.

See also, *American Families of Royal Descent*—Pedigree CXXXIII p. 492 and Pedigree XXI p. 80.

William the Conqueror—m. Matilda of Flanders

Lady Grundred—m. William de Warren

William de Warren, the second,—m. Isabel de Vermandois

William de Warren, the third,—m. Lady Alice

Isabella-Countess of Warren,—m. 4th Earl of Surrey

William, Earl of Warren,—m. Lady Maud

John, 7th. Earl of Warren,—m. Lady Alice de Brun

Wm. de Warren,—m. Joan de Vere

Lady Alice de Warren,—m. Sir Edward Fitz-Alan*

Sir Richard Fitz-Alan,—m. Lady Eleanor Plantagenet

Lady Margarette Mowbray,—m. Sir John Howard

Sir John Howard K. G.,—m. Lady Catherine

Sir Thomas Howard, K. G.,—m. Lady Agnes

Lady Catherine Howard,—m. Rice ap Griffith

Griffith ap Rice,—m. Lady Eleanor

Thomas of Griffith

John Philip ap Thomas

Evan Thomas

Philip Thomas,—m. Sarah Harrison

Samuel Thomas,—m. Mary Hutchens

Samuel Thomas,—m. Elizabeth Snowden

Elizabeth Thomas,—m. Johns Hopkins

Samuel Hopkins,—m. Hannah Janney

Johns Hopkins

Records taken from Bible belonging to Hannah Hopkins (mother of Johns Hopkins). This Bible was presented to Hannah Hopkins by "her son Mahlon Hopkins, A.D. 1835."

("The Bible was presented to the Johns Hopkins University by Mrs. Francis White of Baltimore, January 6, 1912,

* —King Edward the first of England

and is on exhibition in the Gilman Memorial Room, in Gilman Hall.

Births:

Samuel Hopkins jun the 2nd mo 3rd 1759
Hannah Hopkins sen the 19th of 5th mo 1774

Joseph S. Hopkins 28th of 8th mo 1793
Johns Hopkins 19th of 5th mo 1795
Eliza Hopkins the 19th of 5th mo 1797
Sarah Hopkins the 27th of 2nd mo 1799
Hannah Hopkins 11th mo 1801
Samuel Hopkins 11th mo 1803
Mahlon Hopkins 6th mo 1804
Philip Hopkins 31st of 5th mo 1806
Margaret Hopkins 13th of 3 mo 1808
Gerard Hopkins 26th of 11th mo 1809
Mary Hopkins the 8th of 10th mo 1811

Deaths:

Hannah Janney 2nd mo in the 91st yr of her age
Samuel Hopkins the 9th of 12th mo 1814 aged 55 and 6 days.
   Consumption
Gerard Hopkins the 11th mo 14 aged 25 1835 Spinal Affection
Mahlon Hopkins the 2nd mo sd 1840 in the 36th yr of his age
   of anerarithm
Philip Hopkins 23 of 12th mo 1844 in 36th yr of his age
   yellow fever
Joseph S. Hopkins 9th of 2nd mo 1845 in the 51st yr of his
   age bronchitis
Hannah Hopkins died 25th of 11th mo 1846 aged 72 yrs
   A dispepsia
Elizabeth Irwin died 1847 aged 75
Mary Boss died in 1848 aged 61 years of paralysis
Mary R. Congdon wife of Gilbert Congdon died at Provi-
   dence 3rd mo 23 1854
Gilbert Congdon Jr. son of the above born 3rd mo 14, 1854
   died 12 mo 21 1854

IV

"Whereas, By the appropriation already made of a large part of his immense fortune to provide the means of relieving human suffering and of protecting those who are helpless in our midst, and also by his promised munificient endowment of a free university to be established in the suburbs of the city, Johns Hopkins has nobly contributed to the future welfare and happiness of our people, and should receive every evidence of public appreciation and gratitude; therefore, *Be it resolved by the Mayor and City Council of Baltimore,* That the practical and unostentatious charity of Mr. Hopkins, in thus disposing of the wealth which he has accumulated in Baltimore during a life of extraordinary activity, success and usefulness, for the benefit of her own people, has not merely enrolled his name in the list of famous benefactors of mankind, but furnishes the most striking proof of the sincerity and earnestness of his purpose.

Resolved; That the city of Baltimore is proud to record among the many distinguishing facts of her history this crowning act of magnanimity on the part of one of her own citizens, whose whole career has materially contributed to her advancement and prosperity, and whose name has long been known wherever commercial enterprise and integrity are respected.

Resolved; That the Mayor be requested to communicate to Mr. Hopkins a copy of these resolutions neatly engrossed."